FINDING PURPOSE
IN
CHALLENGING TIMES

FINDING PURPOSE IN CHALLENGING TIMES

*My Journey from Refugee to Humanitarian Leader—
and How Anyone Can Rise to Make a Difference*

PATRICK KARANGWA

Legacy

FINDING PURPOSE IN CHALLENGING TIMES
My Journey from Refugee to Humanitarian Leader
Copyright © 2020 by Patrick Karangwa

All rights reserved.
No part of this book may be reproduced, stored or transmitted
in any form without permission, except in the case of
brief quotations embodied in critical reviews or essays.
For inquiries, contact info@ctpbooks.com

First Edition

Published by Legacy,
an imprint of Cotton Tree Press
Washington, DC
Monrovia, LIBERIA
www.ctpbooks.com

Library of Congress Control Number: 2019955968

ISBN: 978-1-7326795-1-1 (hardcover)
ISBN: 978-1-7326795-2-8 (paperback)
e-ISBN: 978-1-7326795-3-5 (digital)

Printed in the United States of America

Map by Ángel Acosta
Photographs by the GHDF media team
Book Cover Design by Angie Alaya
Page Design by Michelle M. White

Our Legacy imprint brings you the stories and wisdom of Africa's changemakers.
If you have a story to tell, or knowledge and ideas to share,
please contact us at legacy@ctpbooks.com.

In memory of my parents,
John Kalegesa and Madeleine Mukandekezi

and

For the refugees, returnees, and
internally displaced persons of this world,
and all who welcome and support them

*"Life's most persistent and urgent question is,
'What are you doing for others?'"*

—Dr. Martin Luther King, Jr.
Civil Rights Activist

TABLE OF CONTENTS

Author's Note	xiii
Uganda/Rwanda Map	xv
INTRODUCTION	1
PART ONE: REFUGE IN UGANDA	7
1 A Boy in Buyongo	9
2 Lessons from My Parents	21
3 Struggling to Survive	31
4 Liberation!	41
PART TWO: RWANDA AT LAST	51
5 Endings and Beginnings	53
6 A Calling	63
7 Tough Start	75
8 A Chance to Grow	85
9 New Direction	95
Photographs	112
PART THREE: A CLEAR VISION	121
10 A Global Reach Begins at Home	123
11 Challenges	135
12 Call to Action	141
EPILOGUE: How to Grow as a Leader and Help Others Rise to Their Full Potential: Seven Keys	147
Acknowledgments	165

AUTHOR'S NOTE

Although this is a work of nonfiction, I have changed the names of some individuals and modified identifying features, including physical descriptions, in order to protect their privacy. Memory is not perfect, and many who could have filled in the gaps are gone, but I have tried to describe the events of my life and work truthfully.

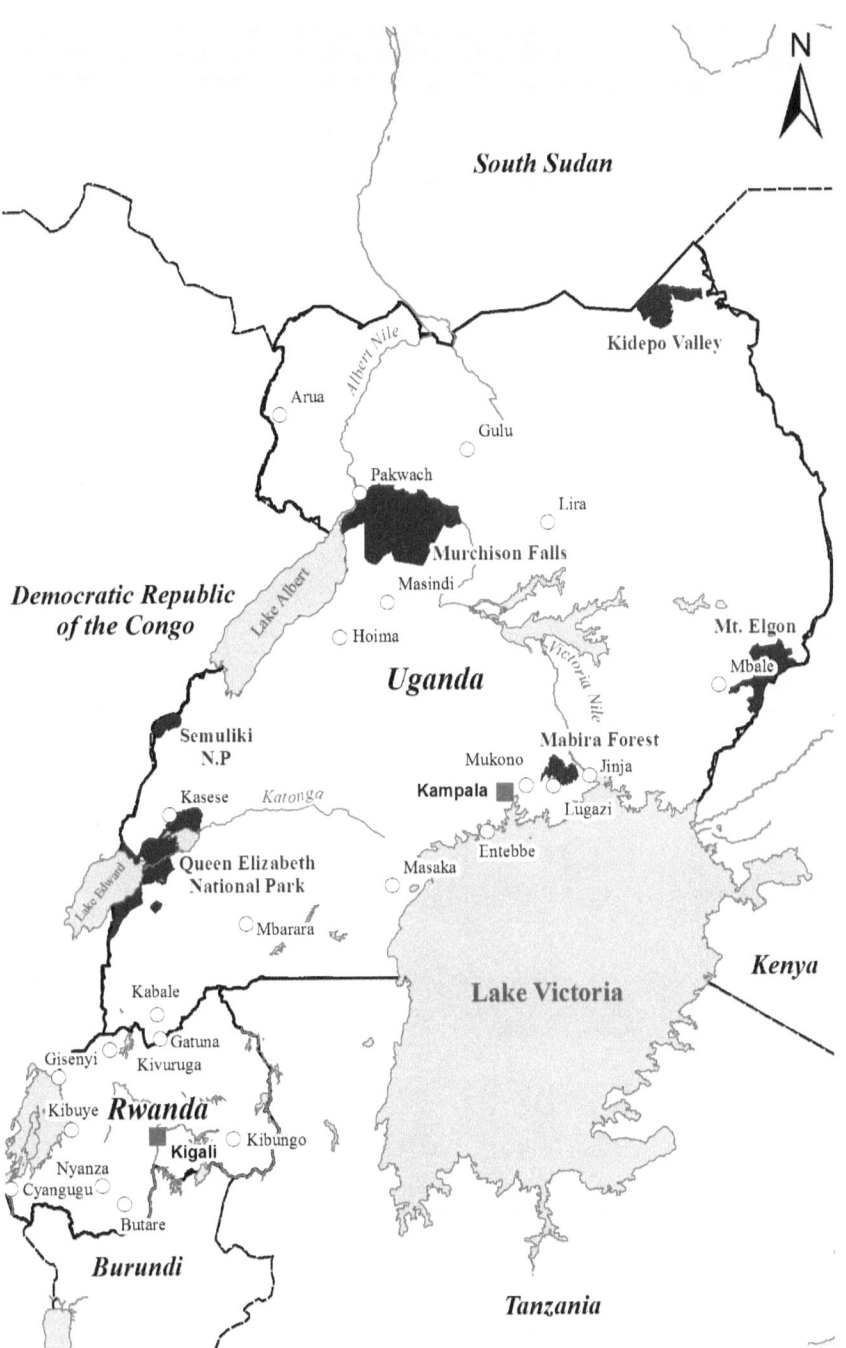

INTRODUCTION

Not long after graduation from university, I got a well-paying job with an international non-governmental organization. Less than two years later, I walked away from it when I got a calling to lead my own organization helping disadvantaged communities. People in my life thought I was crazy to give up what I had, especially for a calling that came to me in a dream. But I was determined to listen to the Rwandans living in communities around me, and address their real and most pressing needs. We were still dealing with the aftermath of the 1994 Genocide Against the Tutsi, and I wanted to promote peace through debate, dialogue, and economic empowerment.

I started the Parlement des Jeunes Rwandais (PAJER) in 2000, and struggled to get it off the ground. The Rwanda Youth Parliament, as it was called in English, is now the Global Humanitarian and Development Foundation

(GHDF) – one of the largest local NGOs in Rwanda. We serve close to one hundred thousand refugees from neighboring countries, as well as vulnerable Rwandan communities.

This is the story of my own time as a refugee, and how the struggles of being a refugee directed my choices and shaped my life. Many of my peers and I were born outside of Rwanda, and most of us are linked today, at the heart and soul, by the similar stories we heard from our parents and the things we experienced first-hand as refugees. We share a profound pain, but, thankfully, we also share a profound triumph. Most of us made it back home in the years following the 1994 Genocide, and are able to raise our children in the place and in the way our parents longed to raise us.

This is also the story of my humanitarian and development work, which has been and will always be God-driven. It has been a long learning process, and now, after close to two decades, I have challenges, lessons, success stories, and best practices to share.

Today, there are close to six million refugees in Africa, and many more people are internally displaced after being forced from their homes because of natural disasters, conflicts, and other circumstances beyond their control. Rwanda, which once sent refugees out into the world, is now host to almost two hundred thousand refugees fleeing conflict in Burundi and the DR Congo. As we strive to develop our nation, these brothers and sisters must be a part of our present considerations, as they will be a part of our future. I believe we are in a unique position to help them with the compassion that is so often lacking in such interventions because many of us have been in their shoes.

Refugees need training in vocational skills so they can have livelihoods, and along with those vocational skills, they need substantial resources to start up, and scale up, their own initiatives. Naturally, when my organization started vocational training we had hundreds of young and energetic applicants who were tired of living on food rations, and thought they could change their lives using the skills they were learning. We find now that many people who are eligible for vocational training don't want to go through it because they see their brothers and sisters who have been trained stuck at a certain level or sitting at home doing nothing because of a lack of capital. The number of applicants to that particular program has decreased by as much as sixty percent and we have lost some momentum. Too many people seem to be giving up.

It's hard to look at someone's face when they've done all you asked them to do, and they need you to take them to that next level where they can sustain themselves, but you can't because there is no funding, inadequate funding, or misplaced priorities. How can I make a difference for more people if the ones I have committed to serving are not being helped adequately? It can be a difficult journey sometimes, but I am a tireless advocate for change. God created us not to be hopeless, but to be hopeful.

My main mission with this book is to encourage you, through my story, to believe in yourself, and know that you can change your life. You can come from nothing, and become something. You can encounter difficulties in your personal or business life, and overcome them. There is a purpose for your life. No matter who you are and no matter your own situation in life, you can also help others and experience the joy and fulfillment such service can bring. To that end, this book is also a call to action. If you have a passion for helping people in need, or even if all you have now is a little willingness to be a blessing to others, God will guide you. If you want to share your personal or organizational talents or resources in some way, this book will encourage and motivate you.

We should always aim to make sure our work impacts others, and so I want to share what I've done, and what I see as the way forward for helping people reach their full potential. The experiences I have had may help others anywhere, even beyond Rwanda's borders. A personal story can lift the spirits of someone who has lost confidence, or lost faith. It can shine light on life's possibilities and bring back hope to people who think they cannot make a difference. A story might even influence someone to step up and do something good, or do something in a more effective way.

There is no easy way to realize a vision for a more perfect world. This is true not only in the humanitarian and development arenas, but also in our personal mission to find or create our life's purpose. The path can be long and hard, but quite rewarding.

Humanitarian initiatives, big and small, offer people an opportunity to serve, to be happy, and to be proud to have done something good in the world. Hopefully, through the story of my journey, you will be encouraged and inspired to start wherever you are, and do whatever you can, to help individuals and communities around you rise above their circumstances. Your service will be a blessing and a legacy you leave behind.

PART ONE

REFUGE IN UGANDA

1

A BOY IN BUYONGO

My father often told us the story of why and how his family left Rwanda. He said he wanted to tell us the truth so we would know we were not living in Uganda by choice, but were displaced.

In 1959, he told us, Rwandans began seeking independence from forty years of colonial rule by Belgium, as well as a change from the Tutsi monarchy that had ruled since the 18th century. Back then, he was a teenager living with his parents in Butare (now part of Huye District), in the Southern Province.

My father and his siblings were well educated because my grandfather, who was not well educated himself, worked for the colonials. When violence broke out and extremists from the Hutu majority started burning Tutsi homes down, my grandparents were able to send some of their children to Belgium for safety. Things got worse a few months later, and to escape the killings that were taking place, my grandparents moved to Congo with the rest of their children, which included my father, John Kalegesa.

Because of the violent transition of political power, which went on until 1962, almost four hundred thousand Rwandans found themselves exiled in Uganda, Tanzania, Burundi, and Zaire (now DRC—Democratic Republic of the Congo). My father and many of his peers came of age in lands that were not familiar, and around people who were not always welcoming.

As the years in exile went by, my father grew into a young man and eventually took refuge in Uganda because he thought he would have better opportunities there.

Both of my parents were from Rwanda, but my mother, Madeleine Mukandekezi, was born in Uganda in the 1930s. Her family experienced a normal migration because they were cattle keepers who moved to Uganda for economic opportunity. Back then, people used to go from one country to another looking for jobs on farms, or looking for green pastures for their animals. Whenever they reached a suitable area, they would build huts made of natural material and make it their temporary home.

My mother, who was the only child of her parents, but one of many children in the household, grew up in this nomadic environment until they eventually bought and settled on a traditional farm. She was educated only up to the primary level because school was not considered important back then. The belief was that education would spoil a child. My mother, like other children, looked after the cattle and stayed close to home.

I don't know how my parents met, but I do know that when they first met each other, my mother lived in a community that hosted refugees, and my father lived in a refugee settlement nearby. Refugee settlements back then, from what my parents told me, were not like the refugee camps we have today. They were more like villages. Small plots of uninhabited land would be allocated to a number of refugee families or individuals, and they would form their own community.

My father's refugee status, and the fact that he was a Francophone struggling to learn English, made his education certificates useless. After numerous failed attempts at getting a good job that would pay well, he decided to do as most refugees did, and go out of the settlement to work on people's farms.

His first job was digging to prepare soil for growing feed for cattle, and crops for human consumption. He and a team of men and women would be given a portion of land to dig with shovels, or, if they were lucky enough to be hired by a well-to-do farmer, with simple wooden ploughs. It could take over a week to dig an acre of land this way. This back-breaking job was often a Work-for-Food arrangement, and my father would occasionally take home either maize, beans, cassava or groundnuts, or a combination of two or three items.

After almost three years of digging, my father got work grazing cattle and other livestock for Ugandan farmers. His task was to keep the cattle from grazing on restricted land, and for this job he usually got paid with money, as well as with milk from the cows.

My father did these farm jobs for a total of seven years before he decided he was going to start a new life in Kampala. To get there, he hitched rides on lorries that carried goods from the village to the city, and paid his way by helping drivers load goods onto their vehicles. Shortly after he got to Kampala, my mother joined him and they got married.

My father continued to do manual labor, farm work, and odd jobs for quite some time because there weren't many good opportunities for refugees in Kampala either. When my three older siblings came along, getting food on the table was a challenge, and as they grew up, getting them access to education was an even bigger one.

My father told us that in those first few years he was desperate and frustrated with the limited opportunities and low wages that caused my three older siblings to miss almost five years of school. At some point, the two eldest were sent to live with our paternal grandparents who were still in the Congo. They left before I was born, and I would not meet them until I was a teenager.

My father was determined to move into a life that was more professional, and eventually, with help from friends, he got a job as an administrator in the logistics office at

Kawolo Hospital in Mukono. Mukono is about an hour's drive east of Kampala. It is a bustling, municipal city now, but in those days it was a rural village, full of banana and sugarcane plantations, with just one road going to Jinja, a city located on the shores of Lake Victoria.

The job in Mukono came with a modest house in the hospital's staff quarters, and my mother got work nearby as an office cleaner. The last of us were born in this phase of my parents' lives, making for seven children altogether. The first-born is Dusenge Inias, and the second-born is Gasenga Yine Gloria. Next is John Bosco, and then me. Because the first two were away, I thought Bosco was my only sibling until my sister, Mbabazi Margaret, was born when I was eight. After her came my brother Mutabazi Joseph, followed by the last-born, Dusabe Maria Goret.

When I was eight years old—long before I heard these stories about my parents' backgrounds—I was sent to live with my maternal grandparents to give my mother one or two years to focus her attention on the new baby, my sister Margaret. I also had an important traditional role to play by helping my grandparents—I called both of them Jajja—in their old age.

My maternal grandparents lived in a simple grass hut with a thatched roof in Buyongo Village, Western Uganda, where forests dominated the landscape. The village was about 200 kilometres, or 125 miles, from Mukono. They didn't have much, but they took good care of me. For my part, I fetched water from the community well, swept the house and yard daily, ran errands for them, and helped to take care of the calves when the cattle were out grazing.

Meanwhile, Uganda was embroiled in a civil war that had started in 1981. Yoweri Museveni, then a political activist who had been involved in helping to topple Idi Amin, was leading an armed uprising against the government of President Milton Obote. Museveni's National Resistance Army (NRA) claimed the elections that put Obote in power had been rigged. As the war dragged on, travel was restricted and I could not go back to my parents when the time came. At some point, we lost all communication with them.

I continued to stay with my Jajja, and, as the calves and I grew bigger, I was promoted to taking them out to graze after school. Because of the war, life was not easy, but we felt lucky and grateful that the school I attended was still open and functioning normally despite the fighting.

I was in Grade 4 at that school when, one day, good news spread through the playground during break time. It was so good I didn't know whether to believe it or not. Back in class, Mr. Ssempala, the homeroom teacher, confirmed it:

"Tomorrow you'll be receiving school supplies, courtesy of the Ugandan government," he announced.

It took about two minutes to restore order to the classroom after we heard exactly what we would be getting: book bags, reading books, large notebooks, pens and pencils, and—what we cheered most loudly for—mathematical sets. A maths set consisted of a ruler, two set squares, a protractor, a drawing compass, an eraser, a small pencil, and a sharpener, all organized neatly in a little rectangular tin. The cost of those sets was prohibitive to poor families like ours. I was even excited about the notebooks we would get. Big, 96-page notebooks for each subject, that would last throughout the year.

I remember running the last kilometer home to share the good news about the school supplies with my grandparents. Their faces lit up with smiles and my grandmother pointed to my khaki uniform pants that no longer reached my ankles.

"Now we can get you new ones," she said.

We all laughed and started suggesting other things we could now afford since the school supplies would be taken care of.

I could hardly sleep that night. I lay on my wooden pallet, the poles barely covered with a mat made of banana leaves that needed to be replaced, and dreamed of those large notebooks. The small 24-page ones were all we could afford, but having two or three per subject was a little bit difficult to keep nicely as a young boy. When you have only one large notebook per subject throughout the course of the year, then you keep your notes well. In a couple of days I was going to be that boy—one with neat, organized notebooks in a brand new bag, and a uniform that fit.

Despite my tossing and turning, I woke up at 5 A.M. the next morning, as usual, to get ready for the long 3-hour walk to school. I lit a wood fire to heat up a pot of water, and after a bath with my bucket outside in the cold morning air,

I put on my khaki pants and my faded blue uniform shirt. I didn't have school shoes back then, so I wore sandals made from tires. They were good sandals, though, because the rubber was strong and my feet had room to grow.

When it was time, I left for school carrying my book bag that was falling apart, and a strong stick to fight off the snakes and wild dogs I would encounter as I walked through the dense forest.

That morning, Satia was the first of my friends to join me on the way. When these things started to matter, I would learn that he was also Rwandan. On this day though, he was simply my best friend.

Satia was one grade ahead of me, and he and I were the only two in the village who went to school consistently. Others attended on and off, and many eventually dropped out for good. Satia was armed with a stick too, and though he was not as poor as I was, he was just as excited about the things we were going to get.

A few other students soon joined us, and the free school supplies was all we could talk about. Even those with parents who were considered wealthy were excited. Wealth in the villages back then was based on the number of cattle you had, how big your family was, and how much land your family owned. That was it. We were deep in a rural village and our living standards were somewhat similar. We all needed those school materials, and if any wild dogs had tried to attack us that morning they would have been very sorry.

We arrived at school by eight-thirty and sat through a couple of classes, probably not hearing a word Mr. Ssempala was saying, until it was finally time to line up for the new school bags that were filled with good notebooks, pens, pencils, and that prized mathematical set. For once, no one had to be reminded to behave and not push. We were on our best behavior because no one wanted to be sent to the back of the line.

The first students who got their bags grinned as they pulled out the treasures at their desks, and those of us still in line looked back and grinned with them, wide-eyed and happy to see everything that was promised. We couldn't help getting a little noisy and pushy as we got closer to the front. Maths sets! Huge notebooks! I was almost bouncing up and down.

When it was finally my turn to get a bag, Mr. Ssempala's frown stopped me in my tracks. He held up his palm as if to ward me off.

"No Patrick, you are Rwandese," he said loudly, in front of everyone. "You are not a Ugandan so you are not a beneficiary of this."

Everyone got quiet. I stood there, stunned, looking up at him and unable to move. Then, turning his eyes away from me he added, "If you want to have access to free education materials, go to the United Nations High Commissioner for Refugees. That's where you belong."

I wanted to cry but I held back my tears and stayed where I was, too embarrassed to turn around and let the other children see the pain on my face. But then Mr. Ssempala shouted again:

"Go back to your seat!"

I turned and went back with my head down. I was heartbroken, and for some reason, I also felt ashamed. I didn't even know what it meant to be a refugee. All I knew was that I was the only person in my whole class who desperately needed those school supplies and didn't get them.

Life as a refugee is one of the most difficult you can ever live. The community that gives you refuge sees you as an outsider, and you are often at an unfair advantage. Where we lived, refugees were usually given short-term jobs and most could never enjoy the security of long-term contracts. Back then refugees were always paid below the minimum wage, or paid less for the same job others did. Even refugee children, as I had found out, were at an unfair advantage.

The incident with the school materials pained me so much that I still find it hard to talk about, and will never forget it. It was a turning point because it made me start thinking about my life and who I was. I was born in Uganda, and until then, if anyone had asked me if I was Ugandan, I would have said yes. When the teacher told me I was not a Ugandan but a Rwandese, that's when I first started feeling I didn't belong.

I ran almost all the way home on the day of the incident, not being able to bear walking with my tattered bag next to my friends who were proudly carrying their new bags. My grandparents were sitting outside waiting for me, and their smiles disappeared when they saw my face.

I was curious and wanted to know more about my situation and what it meant to be a refugee, but my grandparents didn't want to engage me in any discussion of that kind. I was an emotional young boy and took everything seriously, so they tried to convince me that maybe the teacher had simply had a bad night.

Since children weren't supposed to ask too many questions, I was left to my own thoughts. I wondered if I was supposed to go to school or not, and I started to fear that one day I would be treated unfairly in other ways. I was especially worried that if a teacher could do such a thing to me, then maybe tomorrow he could decide not to give me good grades.

Now I know my grandparents didn't want to explain everything to me out of fear that I would feel different and isolate myself from others. They didn't know how long we would be in Uganda, and they wanted me to fit in and remain a part of the community.

Though my classmates were kind, I wanted to get out of that environment, but my grandparents dismissed my fears, pointing out that Mr. Ssempala was the only teacher who caused me grief, and that I might find the same or worse elsewhere. In those days students didn't dare challenge teachers, and even parents were afraid to take the risk of speaking up for their children.

I thank God for Mr. Ssempala now, because I think he helped me in a way that he didn't mean to. I didn't appreciate it in the moment, but his actions made me think seriously about who I was, and what I wanted for my future. If he had not done what he did, I would have been comfortable in that existence—not a Rwandan, not a refugee, but just a boy in Buyongo who had no worries except for having to fight wild dogs on his way to school.

It turned out I would stay in that school for one more year with Mr. Ssempala as one of my teachers, because when the NRA won the war in 1986 and Museveni became President of Uganda, I could not bear to leave my Jajja. They took me home to Mukono as soon as we could travel, but after several months with my parents, I insisted on returning to Buyongo to help them a little longer. They were getting older and I felt they needed me even more.

I probably would have stayed with my grandparents a lot longer than I did the second time around, but a wild dog bit me right after I entered the forest to go to school one day. I had my stick with me, but there were six dogs in the pack, and my friends had not yet joined me for the walk. That dog turned out to be rabid, and I had to go to Kampala for a series of shots. I was in critical condition by the time we got there, and my parents decided to keep me for good this time.

2

LESSONS FROM MY PARENTS

When I was living with my parents in Mukono again, the memory of the incident with the school supplies led me to pay close attention to the advice they were always giving to me and to my siblings.

"You need to have a clear vision for your future," they would say. "You may not have all the basic things that you need, but if you have a clear mission and vision, you can get to where you want to be in life."

At that time I didn't yet have a clear or specific vision, but I definitely started thinking about my destiny, and I knew I did not want my children to have the same type of life I had already lived, or the type of life I was seeing around me in other families. In those days, many parents lost their children because they could not give them the basic needs or the kind of time that children require. The community itself was not always friendly either. A refugee could never be seen as an asset, but always a liability, and one with no rights during the period of displacement. For both children and adults, that was the reality of being a refugee.

"Patrick, you are lucky," my father would say to me. "You were born at a time when I could at least get a little money to pay your fees."

But I would think about the condition of my new school, and ask, "Am I lucky with this type of education, Daddy?"

He insisted that I was. He even said that I was getting the best education. Of course it wasn't the best education, but I understand what he meant now. What he meant was that the ones before me couldn't even go to school. I think he also told that story, and many others, to show the contrast between then and his early life in Uganda. He was always trying to show us that circumstances could change.

Over the years I've come to see how true that is. Circumstances can change for any of us at anytime, and in any direction. And just as wars and natural disasters can devastate lives in an instant, people have the power to improve their own lives, and the lives of others, by making a conscious choice and taking concrete actions to do so. The decision takes only an instant.

I appreciate my parents because, even though we were young, they were open with us and gave us a lot of guidance. They paid attention to everything we did. I remember, for example, the time my father noticed I was home from school early one Friday, and asked me why.

"I left because it's cleaning day at school," I told him.

He stared at me for a moment and shook his head, frowning. "If it's cleaning day, go back and clean," he said.

"Go back right now, and I'm going to check with your teacher to make sure you did your part."

I had to run back to school and make sure my teacher saw me working so I wouldn't get in trouble with my father.

We were living an average life, not rich but not too poor either, and my parents were teaching us, especially through their own example, to be down to earth and do whatever was necessary to keep moving forward in life. We were brought up in a deeply Christian family, and that influenced the way we were raised. Both my father and mother were Catholics and true Christians, and all of us attended every church service as well as any extra teachings offered by the church. I was not too keen on spending so much of my time this way, but as a child, I had no choice.

One thing I did enjoy was family time at home. Every evening we would have dinner together, with the house lit up by old petrol lamps since we had no electricity. My two oldest siblings were still away, so it was just Bosco, me, Margaret, and, later, the two little ones—our brother Joseph and our sister Maria Goret. We would all sit at the table over typical Ugandan food—matoké, ugali, vegetables, sweet potatoes, and either beans or groundnut stew—and our parents would advise us on how we should behave.

My mother encouraged us to be resourceful, and told us we needed to make sure that we worked hard and didn't just sit there waiting for food at the end of the day. Both of them always assured us that we would one day go home to Rwanda, and they wanted us to be sure to go with something to offer.

"Everyone has something to offer," my mother would say. "As long as you have breath in your body, you have something to offer someone who needs help, or something to offer as a service to others."

At that time I didn't know what I wanted to offer my country, but I did know how to serve, and how to be resourceful—especially when we needed money. One thing I did regularly was help with Market Day. My mother grew onions and tomatoes in our small garden, and used to sell them on Market Day, which was every Wednesday. I would join her after school, eager to be part of such a large community activity. Hundreds of people would bring things to sell in the large outdoor space, and many hundreds more came from surrounding areas to buy food and other goods.

Now, the problem was, in our traditional market people with the same goods sit together, so everyone near us had onions and tomatoes to sell. I knew I had to stand out.

"I've reduced the price!" I would shout as loudly as I could. "Please come and buy!"

My boldness was unusual because when I was growing up, most children were afraid for their friends to see them selling things at the market. They would be ashamed, but I was never ashamed. I liked selling.

I was so well known that kids who came to shop with their parents would say, "Patrick is selling onions; let's go and buy our onions from him." Being a young seller at the market helped too, because the shoppers had big hearts for kids.

Besides winning adults over at the market, I also built relationships with our neighbors and did small jobs for them, like fetching water. They would leave me their house keys in the morning, and I would fill up their 20-litre plastic jerry cans at the well after school.

I usually gave all the money I made to my mother. It brought me joy to see her happy with my contribution and to know that it would ease her burdens and improve our lives in some way. One time though, when I was about to go into Grade 7, which in Uganda is the last year of primary school, I decided I had to have my first pair of real shoes. My tire sandals were worn out, and Bata—the global footwear company—was promoting their Back to School shoes, which came with a free pair of good socks.

I didn't know how I would get money for the shoes until, by chance, I overheard a neighbor and her friends complain about the store-bought brooms that weren't good for sweeping outdoors. People living in the staff quarters were mostly middle-class workers and I knew they had no time to go to the bush to cut, dry, and tie their own traditional brooms.

To raise the money for the shoes, I wanted to go into the bush, about two kilometres away, to get palm branches and make those traditional brooms to sell. For some reason my father didn't want me going into this business, but I convinced my mother to advocate for me, and he finally relented. I made and sold brooms until I had enough money to buy the shoes, and both of my parents were quite impressed with my resourcefulness. With what was left over, my mother helped me open an account at the Uganda Commercial Bank, and that was my foray into saving and becoming more self-reliant.

I still didn't know exactly what I wanted to do in the future, but it was in that last year of primary school that I started to think I might want to be a doctor so I could help take care of my parents.

My parents' own mission and vision was simply education for us, their children. In Africa when your parents are well off and they have houses or any other assets, you expect that when they die you will inherit those things and take over the management of them. My father wasn't rich and he had nothing big, but maybe because of the culture and because of the environment in which we lived, we expected him to tell us he was working hard to leave us something. Instead, he told us clearly that our education would be our wealth, and we should expect nothing else from him.

At the time, my siblings and I weren't happy hearing we would get nothing but education, but now I know he gave us good advice and the best thing he could give. We grew up in that spirit of seeing education as wealth, and we have never blamed him for taking that stance. My father knew what had happened to him: His parents were well off in Rwanda and all of a sudden things changed and they lost everything. The only thing he had were the certificates showing the level of education he had achieved, and in the end those certificates eventually did help him get a better job and prosper.

He said to us, "If I didn't have a good education, I would have come here and been a digger or a cattle keeper for the rest of my life, but I knew in time and with perseverance I would get a job that suited my needs and my qualifications."

Education is what protected him, and he wanted to give us the same thing.

"In your journey through life, you will leave behind houses, and you will leave behind land and many other possessions," he said, "but wherever you go, you go with your education."

As teenagers we didn't always appreciate it, but I could understand why my parents were advising and encouraging me and my brothers and sisters every single evening. I knew children who became disappointed and frustrated, and eventually ended up leaving school. I saw young children at adolescence leaving school and becoming drug addicts. Some children would even leave the home of their parents without permission and go into one of the towns to work for Ugandans. There were many young people around us who were going through things that led them to make decisions that were not good for their future.

Some parents would leave their children at home alone and go work somewhere for as long as a week, but we were lucky. We always had one parent close by. My father used to go away for work and spend weeks apart from us sometimes, so my mother left her office job to stay with us all the time. We knew very well that if they were both working it would increase our income and we would have a better life, but they chose to make taking care of us a priority.

My mother stayed home and focused on instilling the right values in us. She brought us up to be able to help ourselves, and to be able to help the family. I remember her creating timetables for each of us so that we would be disciplined and responsible with all that we had to do, and reminding us that no success comes without struggle. "Hard work produces the sweetest fruit," she often said.

As difficult as life was with only one parent bringing in a regular income during that period of my life, I will always be grateful to my parents for choosing to keep a close watch on us and for training us in the way that we should go.

It was in the Mukono house that my parents also instilled in us the importance of culture and traditions. They were in a foreign culture and environment that could have forced them to change their names as well as their way of living, but they were determined to preserve their authenticity. For example, some refugees changed their names to fit into the society, but my parents never did. They kept their given names and were not afraid to give all seven of us typical Rwandan names.

An important part of culture is language, and I thank my father for teaching us ours. "Don't forget about your own language," he always said. "You're learning English, and you're learning Luganda—the traditional language here—but you must also learn Kinyarwanda because we're going home soon."

He was a tough teacher. We had some books written in Kinyarwanda and he made us read them for practice. He also encouraged us to speak Kinyarwanda at home. It was difficult for us because it seemed like we were the only people who were speaking it in the whole community. You could find us asking ourselves, "Why is he telling us to speak this language which no one speaks here?"

Much more fun than the Kinyarwanda lessons were the Rwandan songs we were also learning. We enjoyed them, and would have small singing competitions at home. My parents thought the songs would encourage us to learn more and grow up in that spirit of desiring to go back to our country. They were right. Songs about Rwanda and the beauty and happiness we would find there inspired us to love our country fiercely, sight unseen.

We spent many evenings talking about Rwanda, and sometimes my father would show us videos. He would also invite us to come and listen to the Rwandan evening news, and would translate the many things we didn't understand. We learned a lot of history through him—from the era of Rwanda's monarchy to the Wind of Destruction, as the 1959-1962 revolution was called.

Along with guidance and education, our parents gave us much love, and if they ever had any differences between them, as all married couples do, we never saw it. The loving relationship they had is one that guides my own marriage and family today.

Life in Mukono was good, but soon, as my father had often told us it could, circumstances changed.

3

STRUGGLING TO SURVIVE

Sometime during the last year of my primary education, I came home one day to find my older brother, Bosco, waiting anxiously for me. He rushed to meet me at the gate, and his wide eyes scared me. "Daddy collapsed at work!" he said.

"When? Why? Where is he?" I threw my bag down and wanted to rush off to find him.

"Mama is there. She left three hours ago and said we should wait."

I could hardly bear the agony of not knowing if my father was okay or not. After a few hours that seemed like an eternity, my mother finally returned and told us what she knew. My father was vomiting blood and had been admitted to Mulago Hospital, the best and biggest public hospital in Uganda. His condition was serious.

Eventually, my mother had to spend all her time traveling back and forth to the hospital either to be at my father's bedside, or to take him in as an outpatient. He was in for long-term care with a diagnosis of bleeding ulcers. With no income from my parents coming in, I had to come up with a way to take care of the whole family—including Margaret and my younger siblings who were now away at a Ugandan primary boarding school, and Bosco, who was there at home with us but unable to take on any responsibilities.

Selling tomatoes and brooms was not going to help us this time. I needed serious, steady work. But there was a problem: I was only 13 years old. Luckily, I was quite tall, and perhaps more mature in appearance and behavior than normal boys my age because of the life I lived. A few days after I graduated from primary school, I walked into the Lugazi Sugar Works factory and got a job as a cleaner at the sugar cane plantation. I thought it was something I would do during the two-month holiday while I waited for my exam results for entry into secondary school, and for my father to recover from his illness. We still didn't know just how serious his condition was and how much of a toll his health problems would take on all of us.

In the sugar cane mill, the primary machine used is a crusher that squeezes the stalks of cane to get the juice out. Thousands of particles fly out of the crusher as it's squeezing. My job was to clean the place constantly, because those particles pile up quickly.

If you have seen a blizzard in a country that has winter, that's what it was like. Sugar cane dirt piles up fast and nonstop, like snow in a blizzard, and shoots out of the crusher the way snow shoots out of a snow blower. More than fifty times each shift, while others fed the crusher, I had to gather the sawdust-like particles, put all of it in a wheelbarrow, and take it to the dumping site. Outside the factory I could see that I had worried needlessly about my age; there were other children smaller than I was, working in various capacities.

Working at the sugar cane factory was a hazardous job with a daily risk of occupational accidents. One week I would work the night shift, and then the next week I would do the day shift. The night shift was particularly dangerous because it was easy to fall asleep. If I did, I would find myself being covered by those particles because they were falling fast. A person could suffocate to death if they fell into a deep sleep, and all the workers had heard of cases where that happened in other factories.

One other danger was the extremely high temperature from the nearby boiler. The vats of cane juice had to be boiled at 98°C, or 210°F, for several hours, and the temperature in the room could reach an unbearable level. That kind of heat could cause serious problems. I don't understand how I survived that work, and can only thank God for his protection.

I had worked at Lugazi Sugar Works for a couple of months when news spread in my community that exam results had come in. My friends and I hurried to school to check the lists that had been posted on the wall by the teachers' lounge. I quickly scanned through the K's and found my name: *KARANGWA Patrick: Pass*. But not only had I passed, I had also been given a full government scholarship to Tororo Boys Secondary School.

A scholarship! I jumped up and down, rejoicing, while my friends congratulated me. We were all jumping up and down, congratulating each other with high fives and pats on the back for passing. Our teachers were there too, hugging us and shaking our hands, pleased and proud. My friends and I stayed out celebrating well into the evening, enjoying mandazi, chapatis, and soft drinks.

When I finally got home, I celebrated all over again with my family. My mother had cooked some meat, which was a rarity reserved for special occasions. This occasion was even more special because my father happened to be at home with us rather than in the hospital. As we finished eating, everyone seemed to get a little quieter. I think deep inside I already knew what was coming.

"Patrick, you know we are very proud of you," my father said, looking down at his plate rather than at me.

When he couldn't find the rest of his words, my mother spoke up. "The scholarship is a great blessing, Patrick, but Tororo Boys Secondary is too far from home."

I knew my mother was right. As the main breadwinner in the family, I could not give up my job and go away to attend Tororo. Even though it would mean having to pay school fees, that evening my parents and I agreed I would enroll at the secondary school near home so I could continue helping with household expenses and taking care of Bosco and my younger siblings.

It was tough to resign myself to staying at home, but there were two unexpected blessings: First, I got a partial scholarship that reduced my fees for the local school by fifty percent. Then, sometime during the vacation, my old friend Satia moved from Buyongo to Mukono in search of a job. He found me by asking around, and we soon became the best of friends again.

When school started, my father was no longer going all the way to Mulago Hospital, and was getting regular outpatient treatment at the local Kawolo Hospital instead. From time to time he had to be admitted for short periods due to flare-ups and other complications from his condition, and there was no definite end in sight to his health challenges. At that point my parents were still able to pay school fees for my siblings out of some small savings that they had, and I continued to work for my own school fees, and to get food on the table for all of us. That was the way we divided the responsibilities.

With the demands of secondary school, I found I could no longer work during the day, so I got another job—this time on a tractor that transported sugar cane from the fields to the production unit. I was a turnboy—someone who accompanies the driver and takes care of everything. If the tractor had a problem I had to alert the driver. If it broke down when we went to the field, I was the one who had to deal with arranging the repairs. When the crane had to fill the tractor with sugar cane, I was there to supervise. I was the one who had to do all those jobs, plus the transport, the parking and the offloading.

Much as I was working overnight and on weekends, it was difficult to stretch my salary between my school fees and taking care of things at home. And, of course, our needs at home came first.

One day a friend pulled me aside at school. "Patrick, I see you are tired every day," he said. "I see they are taking you out of class because you have not paid the school fees on time. What's your problem?"

I looked down and kept quiet. I didn't want to tell my story. That was my nature. I wanted to keep my life private and I didn't want to put my stories out there. Satia worked in a factory now, and was the only friend who knew about all the struggles of my life. But this boy asked me again and again, and was genuinely concerned. I finally told him I had to pay my school fees myself, and told him the nature of the work I was doing. He was so moved by what I said, he went home told his parents.

The news traveled fast. Soon, other friends and their parents heard about my struggles too.

One couple had a message for me: "Tell him to come on Saturday and we'll go to our field and give him some cassava." So I went, and these kind people gave me the opportunity, for almost a year, to go in their field and get cassava to feed our family at home. They truly lived out the Bible verse in Leviticus 23 which says, *"When you reap the harvest of your land, do not reap to the very edges of your field or gather the gleanings of your harvest. Leave them for the poor and for the foreigner residing among you."*

We meet a lot of bad people and face many challenges in life, but good people do exist in this world. That couple supported my family in our time of greatest need, and it was all because of a schoolmate who reached out to me.

The times that you have no choice and you find yourself in a certain kind of life, you start to feel maybe that is the life you are destined to live. During that particular time, my siblings and I were all thinking deeply about our father who was in and out of the hospital, and we were worried that he would die. Fortunately, we also had neighbors who were like parents to us. Most of them were my father's colleagues from Kawolo Hospital, and that link is what helped us a lot. They checked on us all the time, asking if we were okay, and encouraging us with prayers that gave us hope for better times.

We were brought up to not be open about our life and so we didn't want to carry our burdens to the neighbors or anyone else, though. "Everything's fine," I'd say cheerfully to anyone who asked about our well-being. But we all lived in small houses next to each other, so they knew I was not telling the truth.

Almost two years after I started working, my father was finished with all treatments and was back home fulltime. Meanwhile, my paternal grandparents had died in the DR Congo, and one of my older siblings, my sister Gloria, had finally come back home. My father did his best to try to get our family back onto its feet, and I continued to work on the tractor for another two years.

When I completed my Senior 4 Ordinary Level exams, I left my tractor turnboy job and went to Kampala to look for work while waiting for the results. My father was back on his feet but he had no capacity to support all of us as he did before his illness, and there were better-paying opportunities for me in the big city.

I soon got a temporary job in Kampala working at the Lugogo Show Ground. Different factories would show their products there on a year-round basis, and an Indian-owned company called Mehta hired me to do some painting. They had me painting high at the top of a building, where the corrugated iron sheets were extremely hot from the sun. I couldn't go up on the roof wearing shoes, and with no shoes on my feet I had to hop around all the time to avoid getting burned. The constant, desperate moving around made it difficult to do the painting. On top of that, the paint would melt and was slippery, so I had a fear of falling.

I had to figure out a way to keep both the job and my life.

After the first couple of days as a painter, I decided I would wake up at five and start the work before sunrise, in order to finish before the scorching noonday heat. Just as I started to put up the ladder, another employee on the site came running.

"Hey! What are you doing?" he asked.

I pointed to the can of paint that I had already mixed.

"It's too early to paint now," he said. "There's still moisture in the air. It will cause the paint to bubble when it dries, and peel off easily."

So, each day, as I slid and hopped around on that hot tin roof, I wondered what would happen if I lost control and fell down. It was a challenging environment and I had no safety nets or medical insurance. I did that painting job for at least a month because it was a big building, and it was only by God's grace that I finished the work unharmed and returned home.

Back in Mukono, everyone was still putting up a strong front, but my father's new lease on life coincided with his mandatory retirement from the job at Kawolo Hospital, and all the money he had saved for this time in his life had gone to pay the medical bills. On a bright, sunny day, when everyone in the neighborhood was out and about, we had to pack all our things into the open back of a large truck and move out of the staff quarters.

The new house was in a congested, lower-income neighborhood not far from the Mukono home I had known all my life. It had one room for all eight of us, with three mattresses on the floor and a curtain to divide the room for privacy. It felt like the end of an era to us, but despite the family hardship, our hearts and minds were soon focused on the hope of a new beginning larger than ourselves: The year was 1993, and, after three years of civil war in Rwanda, a peace agreement (The Arusha Accords) had been signed between the ruling Rwandan government and the Rwandan Patriotic Front.

4

LIBERATION!

The Rwandan Patriotic Front (RPF) was established in 1988 as a political and military organization, but I first heard about it two years later—the year before my father was hospitalized. My parents told us that Rwandans in exile had come together and established this force that would fight to get us back to our country.

In 1986 the ruling Rwandan government, led by President Juvénal Habyarimana, had closed down all discussion of our right to return, so most of us in exile were excited about the RPF while others worried that any fighting would affect family they had at home. It was in October 1990 that the RPF finally marched into Rwanda on their mission.

My siblings and I were still young, but we were overjoyed to finally have real hope that we would someday go to our motherland. My father had fled into exile as a teenager, thinking he would be away just a few months, and here he was, still a refugee years later, now with teenagers of his own. He had seen his own father lose hope when early refugee incursions into Rwanda by the *Inyenzi* guerilla movement were crushed in the 1960s, and he had grown into adulthood desperately hanging on to stories of a glorious past, and dreaming of the day when he would return.

All the Rwandans we knew were happy and eager to do whatever they could to be part of the struggle to get back home. My parents were part of some efforts at the grassroots level, and took this time to remind us that if we did well in school, we would be useful citizens back in our country.

From that period on, and even through my father's illness and the hardships it brought us, I felt a profound sense of pride. I could hold my head up high and say, "I am going to my country, where I have full rights."

The story wasn't mine alone. *We are going back to our country and we are going to have our rights. We are now going to see it!* That was the word in everyone's mouth.

At school, we rejoiced in the fact that in our own country people would never call us Rwandese in place of our names, or with contempt in their voices, and no one would ever tell us we were not supposed to be there. For us boys and girls, the leaders of the RPF were our heroes.

I was curious about the progress of what we called "the liberation struggle", and at home my parents would share the news headlines with us. The RPF's *Radio Muhabura* broadcasts lifted my father's spirits tremendously. "I'm getting old," he would tell us, "and if I get you back to our country and then die the next day, I will die a happy man."

I will never forget that. That was his prayer every single day before he got sick.

When he was admitted to the hospital back then, I remember him saying, "I've been asking God to at least give me a chance to get back to my country with my children, but now I'm going to die here!" When my mother heard this she took us aside and told us, "Whenever you visit your father in the hospital, tell him you are strong and brilliant. Tell him you are grown up and responsible. Tell him about everything that is good in you. Make sure he knows that even if something goes wrong, we are strong and we are inspired by him, and we will realize his dream."

All these situations kept me moving and prevented me from doing things that I knew were not good. Having to work to support my family when my father was hospitalized, and believing we might soon be going home to Rwanda, kept me from falling under peer pressure.

When you are a teenager you want to taste everything. You want to taste alcohol, you want to taste drugs, you want to taste it all. But before every single step that I wanted to take in my life with my friends, I would stop and ask, "Am I fulfilling the dreams of my father?" And then I would think twice. If it would be a bad decision, if it wouldn't help me fulfill the dreams of my father, I would cancel it. That question is still driving me even now. And always, my prayer to God is: *Help me. I'm as vulnerable as any other person.*

I am not always strong, and I can sometimes make mistakes too, and be weak in a way, but I'm committed to making sure I keep my vision and mission moving. I don't want any interruptions that can take me off my path, and that question always brings me back on track. *Am I fulfilling the dreams of my father?* I am still thinking about where I came from, the challenges I passed through with my parents, and the advice they gave me. The lessons I learned drive me along the way even today, and inspire my children too.

Tragically, the Arusha Accords of 1993, which were taking some time to be fully implemented, fell apart on April 6, 1994, when President Habyarimana's plane was shot down over Kigali, Rwanda's capital city, killing both him and the president of Burundi, plus ten others. The Genocide Against the Tutsi began that day, and the RPF resumed their fight. Spurred on by hate messages broadcast from *Radio-Télévision Libre des Mille Collines (RTLM)*, Hutu militias killed almost a million people with machetes, nail-studded clubs and other crude instruments in just one hundred days.

At home in Mukono, we listened to news from Rwanda with heavy hearts that grew heavier as time went on. I don't like to dwell on the details from that period, but I remember my parents were distraught, and we spent a lot of time praying as a family.

When the RPF managed to stop the genocide in July, my father was more determined than ever to return to Rwanda and prepare the way for us to return. One of my childhood heroes, Fred Gisa Rwigema, had been killed early in the war, and the RPF—also known as *Inkotanyi*, which means "Invincible Warrior"—was bent on forming an inclusive government that would unite all Rwandans as one people.

My father left for Rwanda in August, and found the capital city still in a state of chaos. Nevertheless, he was full of hope, and a very inspired man. He had been a refugee for over three decades, and now he was a returnee. He was home, and he felt a great responsibility to play a role in Rwanda's healing and rebirth.

Communication was difficult and we didn't hear directly from my father for a couple of months. There were people moving back and forth between Rwanda and the refugee host countries in the region, so he soon began sending messages and letters to Uganda that way. In one of them he exclaimed that he was even becoming younger. His joking put us at ease and we were happy to know he was doing well. When he finally came back to us in Uganda, we rushed to gather around and greet him. He seemed different to me. Taller and stronger.

"Rwanda has been broken and everything is down to ashes," my father said to us. "But we need to go and rebuild it. I'm ready to take you home."

At the end of 1994, the rest of my family moved back to Rwanda while I stayed behind in Uganda to finish my Advanced Levels. I remained there alone for a few months before my mother came back to get me. Before we could leave, I had to say goodbye to all of our neighbors and our relatives who were staying in Uganda. My mother had said her goodbyes already, the first time she left, but she went with me and wept all over again. Goodbyes were so emotional. You were crying for joy, you were crying for the pain and anguish you had suffered in exile, and you were crying for those you were leaving.

One friend it was hard to say goodbye to was Satia. I tried to encourage him to go with me, but he was moving up in his work at the factory, and said he was happy where he was.

There were many Rwandans staying behind. They were people we had known for many years. Some had settled into Ugandan society and did not want to leave. Others were still wary of the situation at home, and not yet ready to go back. There were many Ugandan families who were close to us, and would be missed as well—especially those who lived in or near the hospital staff quarters, where we had resided for so long. All the goodbyes were emotional partly because we thought we might never see each other again.

In retrospect, I wouldn't say that the whole Uganda experience was negative, or that the environment was always hostile, but a few pockets of people were not so friendly to refugees, and when you're on the receiving end of discrimination those are the things that stand out. I've shared the story of the teacher who denied me school supplies, but there was also the teacher in secondary school—Mr. Bugembe—who would tell me what time staff would be coming around to pull students out of class for being late with fees. I could then plan to slip out and be welcome back to class after that exercise. A majority of my Ugandan classmates were friendly and kind too, and were just as affected as I was when someone treated me harshly on account of my refugee status. I'll always appreciate that.

After the farewells, I packed the few clothes I owned into a small suitcase, and my mother packed our remaining household goods into three bigger ones. We made our way to the Mukono taxi park, where we found transportation to the much bigger Kampala taxi park. It was not hard to leave that house or that neighborhood, and I don't remember looking back.

The Kampala taxi park was crowded with minibuses, people selling all kinds of wares, and hundreds of travelers buying tickets, waiting to leave, or descending from arriving buses. After a long wait, we finally got on the Jaguar bus that would take us to Kigali. It was my first time ever on such a big bus, and it was full to capacity. Most of the passengers were Rwandans going home, and there was a lot of excited chatter—not at all our normal, reserved behavior.

My father used to tell us there was no place like home. He told us our country was beautiful, and that there was no place where you could get opportunities for growth like in your own country. When he told my siblings and me that all the people of Rwanda had one culture, one tradition, and only one language, we couldn't imagine such a thing because in Uganda there are more than fifty clans and tribes who speak more than fifty different languages. Another thing he always told us: "God spends the day in other countries, but he sleeps in Rwanda." As children, we believed him and we desperately wanted to go to the place where God slept. Now here I was, going to that place at last.

During the eight-hour journey, I reflected on what I was leaving behind, and speculated about what lay ahead. I was going to a place I could call home—a place that wanted me. Rwanda not only wanted me, but needed me to help rebuild. I thought about all my father's lessons, and how he and my mother prepared us for this day, and for this time. I was going home with my A-Levels behind me, well educated, resourceful, and ready to aim even higher.

This is the only photo I have of myself as a young man in Uganda, taken when I worked briefly in a florist shop.

PART TWO

RWANDA AT LAST

5

ENDINGS AND BEGINNINGS

It was a long way from Kampala to the border crossing between Uganda and Rwanda, and I kept looking out of the bus window for the first signs of the thousand hills I had heard and sung about all my life. When the hilly landscape came into view, my mouth dropped open.

"Wow! These are *mountains*!" I shouted.

People on the bus laughed, and a man sitting across the aisle said in French, "Le pays de mille collines."

"Land of a thousand hills," someone else translated.

Uganda was mostly flat, so the giant hills that went on as far as the eye could see did seem like mountains to me, and it was clear that people lived and farmed on many of them. I stared at those hills in silence and awe the rest of the way.

When we finally arrived at the Gatuna border post that marked the boundary between Uganda and Rwanda, my mother and I got off the bus and stood in a long queue to go through customs with all the other passengers. There were two buildings on this official crossing point, and customs officers were documenting travelers entering and leaving the two countries.

For the first time, everyone around me was speaking Kinyarwanda. I still didn't speak it well, and whenever I mispronounced a word, people would correct me immediately.

"No, you need to know Kinyarwanda," they would say. "*This* is how you speak this word…"

They were strangers but they took the task of teaching me voluntarily, and seriously. It was a completely new experience and it made me realize I was truly on my way home.

My mother and I got through the immigration procedure easily, and saw that even those Rwandans who didn't have official papers were welcomed and given a *Laisser-Passer* to enter Rwanda legally. We were all going home to a place that wanted us.

We soon re-boarded the bus and drove another two hours towards Kigali. As tired as I was, I kept my eyes open and stared at the scenery along the way: Lush green hills, banana trees, people going about their business of trading goods, small boys shepherding cows, goats grazing unattended, and kids waving at the bus as we passed. I saw more and more buildings as we got closer to town, and, finally, the busy Nyabugogo station, where many passengers disembarked before we continued on.

Most of the buildings in Kigali were still standing, but I could clearly see the scars of war. The buildings looked old and I could see that bullets had destroyed the walls. When we were saying our goodbyes in Uganda, several people had said we were foolish to be going back so soon, and now I wondered what we would do if the fighting started again. I must have looked a little worried, because my mother looked at me and asked, "Patrick, what's wrong?"

"In Uganda the TV news was still showing bodies floating on the rivers," I said. "Are we in danger of being killed as well?"

She took my hand and shook her head. "No, Patrick. The new government has promised to protect all Rwandans," she said. "Everyone's safe now."

Her faith reassured me, and I forgot my fears as we pulled into the taxi park—located where Kigali City Tower is today—and saw Bosco and Margaret jumping up and down and waving at the bus, big smiles on their faces. Others in the same waiting area were waving too, and all of us in the bus were waving and smiling right back. It felt great to be welcome.

To celebrate our safe arrival, we went to eat at a small restaurant in town, which was popular with Rwandans coming home from exile. Later, at the house where my other siblings were waiting for us, my sister Gloria led us in a prayer of thanksgiving to God for everything.

My father was in Kibungo during my first two or three days in Kigali, looking for farmland. When he finally returned, he looked at us, all together in Rwanda at last, and said, "My job is done, and I thank God my dream has been realized. This is the country I was telling you about. If it is bad, you need to make it good, and if it's only good, make it perfect."

I would come to take that mandate very seriously.

It was a shame that our country had gone through such a difficult period of Genocide. Everything had been reduced to rubble, and my family was living in an abandoned house in Remera, a suburb of Kigali. There were abandoned houses everywhere in the city as so many people had been killed or had fled the violence. For those who were returning, you simply had to search for accommodation. If you went to a house and found a sign that said this house has an occupant, then you would proceed and look for another one. That's how things used to work.

Returning home was both joy and tears for us. We were joyful to finally be in the land of my father's birth, but sad because almost all the family members who stayed behind had been killed, as well as two relatives who had returned to Rwanda at some point. Another relative had survived to tell the story because she managed to escape with the help of neighbors who took her in the dark of night through Nyamirambo and to the Mille Collines Hotel, when it was considered a safe haven for Rwandans and foreigners in Kigali.

Hearing graphic stories of the genocide and of the survivors' struggles was difficult in those early months, on top of all the other challenges you would expect. It was also during this period that I finally met my eldest brother, who had grown up with Gloria and had joined the RPF army after our paternal grandparents died.

Being on Rwandan soil for the first time felt like the beginning of my life, and it was definitely the beginning of a spiritual renewal. Today I'm closer to God than I was many years ago. Back in Uganda I couldn't understand why he would let us struggle the way we did. I used to ask, "Why are we here God, if you love us so much?" I became a much stronger believer when I came to Rwanda because I saw this country rising from ashes. Only God could do that, and he would eventually play a big part in my own growth and transformation as well.

I shared a small room with Bosco in that abandoned house for about a year, while we all worked and saved money to buy a home of our own. My Jajja came to live with us around this time, and were happy to be in Rwanda after all these years. He had left in the 1940s and she was seeing her home for the very first time. Being in Rwanda was a dream come true for them, but most importantly, we were all together as a family for the first time in history. When people grow old, affection for their grandchildren increases, so they loved being around us and we loved having them there. That's the memory I have.

At a family gathering in June 1996, my father repeated his declaration that he would die a happy man since his dream of bringing us home had come true. He died a few months later, only two years after our return. His path, his vision, had been to keep us alive, guide us in the way that we should go in life, and get us home so we could develop and enjoy Rwanda. I wish he could have lived long enough to see us developing our own paths and achieving our own dreams. It is one of the things I think about when I sit alone.

My grandparents did not live much longer after my father died. One died in 1997 and then the other in 1998.

Their passing was devastating for me especially, because after living with them in Buyongo for such a significant part of my life, we had a special attachment. I even used to call them my parents, because they were the first parents I knew well. One thing that pains me even up to today is that they died before I had the potential to support them. They loved me and worked hard to help me as a young child, but I couldn't do anything for them because they went when I had nothing to offer except prayers and a hand to hold as I walked beside them.

Despite the pain of our losses, returning to Rwanda was the turning point in our lives as a family. We all found ways to grow and to contribute. Gloria got married and became a caterer, and Bosco eventually chose to go back to Uganda. For my part, I got a job teaching English at Inongo Primary School in Kanombe. It was a 45-minute walk from our house, and I took my youngest siblings, Joseph and Maria, to study there, because their tuition could be discounted and taken out of my 22,000 Rwf per month salary. While working, I also repeated the A-Levels at Lycée de Kigali. I thought it was important to get those credentials in Rwanda so that I would maximize my chances of getting a scholarship to study at a Rwandan university. My future was in this country, and not in Uganda.

After I finished the A-Levels for the second time, I left the teaching job and participated for several weeks in *Ingando*—as our national civic education program was called at the time. Ingando has evolved over the years, and today it's known as *Itorero*. It was there, at the end of 1999, that I learned all about reconciliation and peacebuilding, among other things. When the training was over, I became more focused on what was happening around me and started to think seriously about what I could do with my life, and what I could do for my country. I had been reading books and articles about Nelson Mandela and other great Africans, and was inspired to make a difference in the lives of others. My dream shifted from becoming a doctor to becoming a lawyer or a community advocate, because rather than cure sickness brought on by poverty, I wanted to prevent sickness by fighting poverty. What would I study?

In the end, when it was time to apply for a scholarship from the Rwandan government, I had only three academic options. Most African governments give scholarships for training in areas where they need professionals, and in this case the choices were Economics, Business Management, and Education. Personal preference is sometimes solicited and taken into consideration, and I listed Economics and Business Management as my top two choices, in that order. When I received the scholarship, however, it was to attend the Kigali Institute of Education (KIE), where I would study to earn a teaching degree.

"What's this I'm hearing?" my mother asked, when she found out I was considering forfeiting the scholarship.

"I want to follow my dream of helping the poor," I told her.

"Patrick, you have no more time to waste!" she said. "This country needs you. Take up the opportunity to finish your education, and God will guide you."

As much as it wasn't my first choice, I agreed that the scholarship was a privilege and an opportunity—even a gift from God—because without it, it would have taken me two years or more to earn money for a program I truly wanted, and I may not have managed to do it at all. The education was free, and would give me the prerequisite I needed to go to university later for a Master's degree of my own choosing. So I indeed took up the opportunity to become a teacher, an occupation that had never been part of my dream. Sometimes I believe in destiny. There are many roads that can take you where you want to go, and now I can see that was the way for me.

In March 2000, Paul Kagame was elected president of Rwanda, and I enrolled at KIE, still full of the energy and sense of possibility I got from the Ingando experience. Genocide trials had begun in 1996, and by the time I started university there were over one hundred thousand suspects awaiting trial. There was also a lack of peaceful coexistence among people in the communities. Many had relatives who were perpetrators of the genocide, and many had relatives who were victims or survivors. At the university in those days, you could find on the latrine walls, hateful words and threats about finishing the killing. It was traumatic for people who were still remembering those who had died.

At KIE I was surrounded by students who were going to be leaving after four years of university to work in government offices and the private sector, and I thought if they were experienced in reconciliation and peacebuilding, they would be good seeds that would help us grow into a prosperous society and nation. I wanted to rally them together and do something in that area. A few of my fellow students were on board with my idea and joined me to start up what we called the Student Club for Unity and Reconciliation. Deogratias Rwangisa, my vice chair, was instrumental in helping me get the organization off the ground. SCUR, as we called it for short, soon started operating with the main objective of facilitating peacebuilding and reconciliation among Rwandan youths at the universities and in secondary schools.

When the Gacaca courts began in 2001 as a way to speed up the judiciary process, we at SCUR found ourselves organizing dialogues to help young people understand what was going on. Gacaca was an old, community-based system of handling conflict and disputes, and had been revamped to help bring the truth of the genocide to light, and restore the country's social fabric through both punitive and restorative justice. As the trials went on, we wanted our fellow students to see each other as colleagues and friends, and not punish each other for what their parents and relatives did, or for who their parents and relatives were. We also had to raise awareness that not every person from a particular clan was a perpetrator of genocide.

With our student club growing fast, I went to the National Unity and Reconciliation Commission (NURC) to get support for our work. NURC had been established just the year before, in March 1999, to promote unity and reconciliation among Rwandans and to eradicate division and discrimination. They connected us to GTZ, who was the primary donor in the reconciliation arena. (GTZ, the German Technical Cooperation organization, is now known as GIZ—the German Society for International Cooperation). GTZ started funding us, and soon sent us additional support in the form of an Eastern European exchange student named Marcine. It was Marcine who taught us that what we had been calling "debates" were actually dialogues. He taught us how to organize proper debates, and then we formed a team of Trainers of Trainers to help start debate programs in many other schools. Over time we saw many changes in the students and the schools, including an end to the hateful writing on the walls.

As for me personally, the work I was doing with SCUR and the difference we were making in the way people interacted with each other began to feel more and more like what I was meant to be doing with my life.

6

A CALLING

Between studying at KIE and running the Student Club for Unity and Reconciliation, life was quite busy. On top of that, I had a part-time job teaching at St. Mary's School in Kimironko, a suburb of Kigali, to help support my family. In my third year, I left the job at St. Mary's and applied to do a formal internship at Green Hills Academy—one of the best private schools in Kigali. There were three candidates from KIE vying for the internship, and the headmaster of Green Hills, a Canadian gentleman, gave each of us a prerequisite to complete. Mine was to study the soil and the layout of the school grounds, and come up with a plan for landscaping.

Oh my God, what is this? I asked myself, surprised.

The other two candidates got their assignments, and we all left with orders to return in two days to present our work and recommendations.

I knew I wasn't qualified to advise the school on soils and plants, but I decided I would use common sense and ask myself what I would do if it was my home. I surveyed the environment, did some research on plants to see which ones would do well in our climate and on sloping hills, and then I put a written presentation together.

When I arrived at the appointed time two days later, I was the only candidate there. When I called my colleagues they said weren't coming because they didn't apply to do random work – they applied to practice teaching.

I handed the headmaster my presentation and he set it on his desk without even glancing at it.

"Patrick, I'm not going to read your presentation because I don't expect you to advise us on our landscaping," he said. "What I wanted was to see if you are ready to take up difficult tasks and challenges in your life. Your friends are lazy, but you passed. Welcome to our teaching staff."

The internship lasted one term, and when I graduated from the Kigali Institute of Education, I was offered a full-time job at Green Hills Academy, teaching biology. I liked teaching, but I didn't feel passionate about it. I had other interests I wanted to explore, and I kept on looking around to find opportunities that would help me achieve my dream of advocating for the poor and other disadvantaged people.

One day, during the holidays after that first school year, I opened up a newspaper and saw an ad seeking a program development officer for the Coexistence Network. The project was to focus on reconciliation and development, and it was being implemented by Norwegian People's Aid (NPA). The ideal candidate was required to have at least three to five years of experience in the development field. I had zero years of experience. Another requirement was a degree in social sciences, education or development studies. I had the degree in education, and that gave me confidence. I said to myself, *Let me try...Who knows?*

During the competition for the job, there were other applicants who had ten to fifteen years of experience, even more. I heard them talking when we were sitting for the interview. These were qualified people, and I knew my chances were slim. When I recognized a couple of them as well-respected people from well-known organizations, I didn't think I had a chance at all. I wanted to withdraw my application and just go home. I almost gave up, but I needed a job badly, and this one would give me a chance to work in an established organization that was making an impact in people's lives. I had been called to the interview, and so I was going to see it through. My thought was that it would at least be good experience for future interviews.

A few days later, I stared at the shortlist in astonishment. I was one of the top three candidates! We were invited to come back and work together on a task, and after that, we were interviewed again. On the day that the interviewers had said they would let us know, I stayed close to the phone and jumped every time it rang. Finally, sometime in the afternoon, I got the call from NPA's Department of Human Resources. The job—unbelievably—was mine.

"Patrick, how did you make it? We know you! Just fresh from school! How did you get the job?" These were the questions and comments I heard later from my colleagues.

There was an older man, a fellow applicant, who saw me at the office soon after, and congratulated me. He was working with the National Unity and Reconciliation Commission, and was the main one whose presence at the interview made me feel like I was out of my league. He had a different question for me: "How come *I* failed?" he wanted to know.

Honestly, I was shocked too. I couldn't believe I had beat out all those experienced people. I had said let me give it a try, and I gave it a try. Success came because I had tried despite the odds. In hindsight, I believe an often-told story about my grandfather influenced me, in a subliminal way, to take that leap:

When we were refugees, my father had tried hard to encourage us to make the best of our situation and prepare to go back to Rwanda. That seemed like an impossible dream to me. I often doubted him and told him so. At those times he would tell us stories of others who had come from far—from deep in the villages sometimes—and ended up succeeding. One of those success stories that my father told us was about his own father. He said that when my grandfather was a young man, struggling and unemployed in his village, he decided to ask the colonial masters for a job on their coffee farm, and approached the Belgian in charge.

"No, you don't speak French so you are not fit to work with us," the Belgian said.

My grandfather was not discouraged. "If you give me a chance, if you give me one day in the office, I'll speak French," he said.

The Belgian laughed. "No, you cannot do it," he said.

But my grandfather persisted. He wanted to show this man that if you give someone a chance, they could succeed.

A local peasant insisting that he be given a chance intrigued the Belgian in charge, and he said, "Okay, I'm going to give you a chance for one day."

On what the colonial thought would be his one and only day in the office, my grandfather learned how to say his first word in French. When he had an opportunity to see the Belgian, he said *"Bonjour* – Good Morning!" It was just one word, but the man was impressed. He hired my grandfather to work with them, first as a picker, and eventually as a supervisor at their coffee farms in Butare, Nyanza District. That is how my grandfather became a prominent person who was able to educate his children both at home and abroad.

Stories like that gave us hope and kept us moving. They told us that as poor as our conditions were, if we worked hard and made use of available opportunities, we could rise out of the challenges and problems.

My father used to tell us repeatedly how our grandfather worked hard, and how he believed in himself even in difficult and challenging environments. He was a peasant who had demanded a chance to earn a livelihood, and when the Belgian gave him that opportunity, it was not because he knew my grandfather would learn French in a day, but, as the Belgian himself later explained, "If a peasant can stand up for himself, and take a chance and tell you he is willing to do what it takes, then he's someone who is valuable."

And it's true.

That story about my grandfather gave me a belief that I can be myself, do anything I think about doing, and make an impact in society. This was the spirit that led me to come out on top at that intense job interview, and even today, it is the same spirit that drives me in everything. I know I'm not the best at everything, but I know I can try.

You have to believe in yourself and you have to be willing to put in the effort it takes to be the best. As I employ staff today, I look for people who are motivated and know they can make a difference if given a chance. I tell that story about my grandfather to my own children. I tell them they can be anything. I tell them they can get to the heights of anything, just like their great-grandfather, so long as they believe in their dreams and in themselves, and take the action necessary to make those dreams come true.

When I got the job at Norwegian People's Aid, my father told me, "This is a path that's going to lead you somewhere. Stay on it and keep on moving."

I started working, and I knew nothing, honestly, but I had one of the best supervisors in the world. Marco de Swart is Dutch-Caribbean, and he was one of the people who had interviewed me. He was a young professional who was passionate about his work, and taught me quite a lot. He was patient and always saw potential in me, which I didn't always think I had. He would tell me not to look at the mistakes made, but to look at the potential, and to understand that making mistakes was a natural part of my work. Both Marco and his wife, Petra, who worked for SNV, the Netherlands Development Organization, played key roles in helping me grow and develop professional skills. Their doors were always open, and because of their belief in me, I made progress and was determined to never disappoint them.

I worked extra hard at my job at NPA, staying long after working hours, and doing extensive research to make sure I fully understood what I was doing. My generous salary was helping to support my mother and my siblings, and several other family members too. I was doing well, and everyone at home was happy.

But I wasn't.

At that point in the project, we had worked on the strategic plan for the organization, and it was full of great ideas to promote peace and reconciliation. I think the approach, as with some development organizations even today, was top-down rather than bottom-up. The donors wanted to focus on peace and reconciliation because they felt that was what Rwanda needed most after the genocide. Out in the rural communities, however, the Rwandan people kept telling us: "We are poor. Can you bring us together with some type of economic empowerment program?" Those who spoke up explained that peace and reconciliation would come naturally if they first had such a program in place.

I knew we were not going down the right path by insisting on reconciliation first, before implementing development projects that the communities desperately needed. I felt it would be best to listen to the people, but the recommendations I gave in my project reports didn't change anything, and I didn't speak up.

I grew more and more unhappy with how things were going in the field, and sometimes, despite Marco's mentoring, I felt insecure about my low level of experience. I was not overly zealous in terms of faith, but I was a believer and I would pray about it. I could see that God was helping me make progress in my life, but like many other human beings, I felt the progress was too slow. As humans we always want things to be quick. We want to get there quickly, and we want to get things immediately. I was quite conflicted. I had a good job, and yet I was not happy. I was making much more than I did as a teacher, and yet I was not happy. I had the best bosses and managers, but month after month my morale was going down.

All I could do was continue to pray.

Then, one night, about a year and a half after I started at NPA, I had an extraordinary dream. In the dream a voice said: "You need to move on, because this is not the right place for you. There is something else you need to do." It was like God was talking directly to me, loud and clear.

I thought about the voice when I woke up, but considered it a dream like any other. That night though, the dream came again. This second time the voice was much more powerful and urgent. I could clearly hear a voice telling me, "You need to do something else. You are not happy, and you need to move out of that position. You can do something better." When I woke up it was still very early, around four in the morning. I said to myself, *There is no question about it, and there is no other voice I am waiting to hear. This is the voice.* I decided to listen. I felt I had no choice. And then I prayed aloud and said, "God, guide me and make it clear that this is your voice."

When I told Marco that I wanted to leave, he was taken aback.

"Patrick, why?" he asked, gripping the handles of his chair and leaning towards me.

"When I got this job I thought it would be to my satisfaction," I said, "but I am not satisfied."

"Can I increase your salary a little bit?" he asked.

"No, I'm satisfied with what I have, especially since I never even expected to be a part of this organization," I said. "If you can make increases, do it for the whole team or where you think it is needed."

"Then what is the problem?" he wanted to know.

"I have to do something better," was all I told him. I didn't speak up and tell him what I was thinking, so he didn't know why I wasn't happy with my job. I didn't want to go into specifics about the needs we were not meeting in the rural communities, because I assumed he had no power to change things either, and was only implementing what his boss wanted.

Marco said, "Patrick, you are crazy. This is the right time for you to set up your profile and build your credibility, but you are leaving!"

"Yes, I know," I said, "but it's time for me to go."

The head of NPA, a Norwegian woman with decades of experience in the development field, called me on the evening of the day I left, and invited me out for dinner at The American Club which was situated in the 5 Swiss Hotel in Kiyovu. As soon as we sat down, she said, "Patrick, tell me, why are you resigning from your job?"

"It's a calling," I explained. "I took this decision because I had to, and I'm convinced I'll go out and make a real difference in people's lives."

But even though she believed in me, she couldn't believe in that calling. Like Marco, she also asked me not to be crazy. "Please keep your job," she pleaded. "If you go out there on your own, you'll starve."

"I don't think I even have $200 in my account," I admitted. "I know I'll go through difficult circumstances, but I went through difficult circumstances at a very young age, so now, at this age, there is nothing I fear."

Resigning from my good, stable job seemed crazy to most of the people in my life. Around that time, my beloved sister Margaret was battling a cancerous tumor in her knee, and I had been in a relationship for almost a year with a beautiful and humble young woman I wanted to spend the rest of my life with. Aline Kaneza and I had been introduced to each other by our parents, and had fallen in love over lunch dates at *Le Printemps*—a popular restaurant in Kimironko. I was about to ask for her hand in marriage, so I needed stability more than anything at that point, but I resigned from NPA because it was a God-driven decision. It was a clear calling that came in a recurring dream, and I was willing to trust and obey.

After I resigned from my job at Norwegian People's Aid, I initiated an organization called Parlement des Jeunes Rwandais (PAJER). The English translation is Rwanda Youth Parliament. PAJER was going to be a platform where young people could speak out about the issues of our day. With my own organization, I knew I could do whatever I thought was good. I also felt I could engage those who were in need better than I could if I was working for a big institution that already had structures in place. At NPA, I could not change anything. After all, who was I? Only a junior staff member.

By starting up my own organization, I would have the opportunity to design programs, make changes where necessary, and make sure people's true needs were met. The people I had seen in the rural communities were praying to God for a way out of their dire situation, so my intention to meet their needs, and the needs of others like them, was strengthened by the voice I had heard urging me to move on and do something better. By following my calling, I felt I would be an instrument in a plan much bigger than my own.

7
TOUGH START

I spent my first year as a social entrepreneur setting up the Rwanda Youth Parliament as an official, registered entity, and finding an office. I used my savings to pay the first three months' rent for an office that was just big enough to hold my small desk and chair. My other expenses were transportation, printing costs at internet cafés, and, eventually, a computer so old it would take thirty minutes or more to save something to a floppy disk. Sometimes I would press *Save* and go to lunch, come back, and find it still saving. Without an income, there was a time when I couldn't pay my rent for four months in a row, but luckily, my landlord was sympathetic and patient with me. I had no projects and no money, but I had no regrets about branching out on my own either.

Though he was not happy about me leaving NPA, my former supervisor, Marco, was supportive of what I wanted to do with PAJER, and had offered to help me in any way he could. One day he called and asked if he could come and visit me at my office. He came and sat with me, and gave me all sorts of useful advice. The first suggestion was to get others on board. He advised me to make sure my leadership structure was clear, clean, and progressive, and, most importantly, that it would create meaning for everyone involved. He emphasized that a board of directors should have clear responsibilities, no conflict of interest, be active, and be able to help and represent the organization. He talked to me about commitment, overcoming challenges, writing proposals, and a number of other things. Still feeling "fresh out of school" and like I knew nothing, I wrote everything down with the intention of following all of it.

What I wanted most was to set up a debate program for boys and girls in every one of Rwanda's districts, and then organize major competitions first at the provincial level, and then at the national level. I wanted to replicate the active debate clubs we had in the university because I knew from experience that participating students would see a significant increase in their ability to research and to think critically. Debate was an educational tool, but it also developed a culture of speaking out, and an attitude of tolerance. A good debater learns to tolerate ideas, even if those ideas may not be something they agree with. In a society where we had come through many difficulties, every word you said meant a lot, and I felt those skills and attitudes would be important in the post-genocide situation.

But starting up an initiative can sometimes be a difficult thing. For organizational setup, you need serious funding if you want to have your ambitious programs moving. Now, who will give you funding when you're new in the field? Who will fund a young person who has big dreams, but less than two years of experience in NGO work?

Donor organizations hardly ever give funding unless you have a profile. And to have a profile means you need to have some projects that have been running with some measure of success. You need to have some audit reports, and books of account. In the beginning I had nothing at all. It was one of my biggest challenges. Potential donors were impressed with the ideas I put down in writing and shared in discussions, but their lack of confidence in me was understandable. I had done nothing yet. They couldn't risk funding someone without a profile. That was the challenge and the catch: How could I build a profile without funding? Who would be ready to risk working with me?

While I kept looking for major funding, I decided to at least start something at the local schools around me. At first I thought of organizing debates between schools in the city, but even that was not possible without funds. A simple debate program within a school, however, didn't require funding. It mainly required the will, and a lot of traveling time. I used to walk long distances from my home to the schools, but it was worth it. I got some recent graduates to volunteer with PAJER, and although we agreed with the schools that we would be doing the debates as an extracurricular activity, we organized interclass debate competitions as well. We worked with students in secondary school—Grades 10 to 12—and they were always excited to use the debate platform to speak. Hundreds of students became a part of the program and made time for it.

After a few months, the debate program was going well, but I still had no income. Just when things were at their toughest—and that luck with my landlord was about to run out—Marco called again.

"Patrick, how are you surviving?" he wanted to know.

I laughed and told him I was struggling, but also moving along with my plans.

Then he did something amazing. He offered me a sort of partnership that would help **NPA** programmatically, but also, because of the income I would earn, would help **PAJER** carry out the debate program on a larger scale.

"You were one of my best staff," Marco told me, "and I know your capacity well. I know what you are trying to do, and I believe in your cause."

To me, that was a sign from God, showing me that I was on the right path. Even in difficult circumstances, God was making a way, and the offer from Marco further strengthened my belief that what I was doing was my calling.

I started the year-long partnership with **NPA**, and my monthly pay was almost the same as I earned when I was working as a full-time staff member. There are many things you can do to help people on a small scale, but if you want to start something that requires major funding, the key is to start with what you have. I had initiated the work at **PAJER** with my ideas and my time, then I was able to bring on recent secondary school graduates as volunteers. Now, out of the salary I was getting from **NPA**, I could afford to hire a young man to help me. John Ishimwe had a degree in project management, as well as skills in proposal writing.

He managed the volunteers, and eventually became a debate trainer as well.

With more people on board and with a little money to spend, PAJER was able to reach out to more schools and to out-of-school youth as well. We also got other organizations like Never Again Rwanda and AJPRODHO—a youth association for human rights promotion and development—to put debate into their activity plans. We thus expanded our partnerships and impact without having to spend extra money.

When you are starting out, you need to be committed to your work, strive for good results, and create impact with minimum funding. You also have to move quickly when there is an impending crisis, and I soon had the chance to immerse myself in this lesson after a particularly popular debate between out-of-school youth on the topic, "How Can Youth Improve Their Welfare?" After the event, the speakers raised a number of things that served as a wake up call to me.

"We're not in school, and you are asking us to debate," one of their spokesmen said. "Yes, we will debate because we have many issues to debate about, but are you going to respond to some of these issues?"

Another outspoken young man was more specific. "We don't have jobs. We need economic opportunities. We need to start our own businesses. What do you think about that?"

I agreed with them, but I had no way to support them at the time. The important thing is, they had spoken and I was listening. I had heard.

From that point on, when I met with potential partners, I told them: "We are doing some good work. We're doing debates with the youth, and some of the things that they bring up every single time are crucial. They say they need jobs. They need to start businesses, to be supported, and to be trained. How do we support some of these issues that are outlined by the youth during our debate programs?"

I knew if we didn't get help, a time would come when the students would ask, "Why do we even need to debate anymore, if we've been bringing up issues that are important to our community and there is no response to them?"

The lack of major financial support to meet these economic needs was one of the biggest challenges I had as a manager. We could run the debate program on small funds, but needed much more if we were to help our debate participants and their audiences learn new skills and start small businesses. Without economic empowerment programs to meet the needs of the young people in the community, PAJER would lose its relevance and meaning.

I was still in the stage of searching for funds when Aline and I got married. The organization was struggling, and here I was starting something else on quite a different level. I thought it was the right time, though, and it was a blessing too, that at least one person was willing to risk forming a partnership with me. It's rare to find a life partner who shares your mission and vision, but God answered my prayers in this area, and Aline has been a part of my journey in development and humanitarian work from the beginning. In 2007, almost a year after our wedding, my sister Margaret lost her battle with cancer, and my mother passed away unexpectedly, only a month later. Neither of them lived long enough to see Gisa, our first-born. These were tough losses for me as a young man. It was my new family, and the desire to make a difference in the lives of others, that kept me moving forward. I was also more determined than ever to fulfill the dreams my parents had for me.

By the time my partnership with NPA ended, they had developed a youth empowerment initiative, and I had the opportunity to apply to them for funding. PAJER received a grant to support students in the debate program with peacebuilding and reconciliation activities, and to help those young people start their own businesses. Finally, I could see light at the end of the tunnel. That's how it happens when you have faith. You may move in darkness at first, but all of a sudden you start seeing some stars, some light.

With that grant from NPA, we were able to take our debate program to Rubavu District in the Western Province. Rubavu is situated on the shores of Lake Kivu, and shares a border, and the lake, with the DR Congo. First we did a baseline survey of economic potential in the community so we could link basic entrepreneurship training to viable business opportunities, then we set up a mutual fund to help our debate program participants start small businesses. Besides the many types of businesses that could support the needs of citizens coming from Gisenyi (Rubavu's capital city) and neighboring towns and districts to buy goods, we found a need for making bricks and collecting sand for construction sites. Gisenyi is a popular beach resort town, and at the time it was being developed rapidly. The PAJER team taught the debate participants how to write business proposals, and encouraged them to get money from the mutual fund to invest in building their businesses. The agreement was they would then pay it back with five percent interest. The interest was not for PAJER, but to boost the mutual fund.

It was exciting to see the businesses the young people came up with. One young man planted a field of Irish potatoes that grew extremely well in the mineral-rich soil in that part of the country, and he was able to pay back the money easily. Another young man started a bicycle repair business. He used the money from the fund to buy materials, and then outsourced the repair work to people with the necessary skills. One young lady decided to sew and supply school uniforms. This business was profitable, and she also paid back the loan as promised.

Unfortunately, despite a few successes, this first attempt at economic empowerment of the youth in our programs failed. In the beginning they were paying back the loans, but soon, some of them started defaulting. In most cases it was not because their businesses failed, but because they had no real stake in the fund. They saw it as money that had been given by the donor to help them freely. In the end, the money was a source of conflict within the group, and they wanted to divide what was left among themselves. The lesson we learned from this experience is that free money is not valued or respected. It was a hard lesson, but one that would lead us to success later.

For the next year or so, I supported the organization in every way I could manage, and had a few friends who helped by giving us 100,000 or 200,000 Rwandan francs every now and then for the ongoing debate program. Back then 100,000 Rwf was about $200, and their donations were a lifeline that kept me going until the next big opportunity.

8

A CHANCE TO GROW

The power of debate is that it can impact the lives of participants in significant ways when the topics are relevant. PAJER was using debate as a medium to communicate messages to youth about health, HIV, sexually transmitted diseases, unemployment, sustainable energy, and other topics potential donors and partners were addressing in their own ongoing programs. These topics were particularly relevant to development efforts in post-genocide Rwanda, and our program caught the attention of DED—the German Development Service.

DED program staff visited us in one of the schools in Kigali, and could clearly see the value in what we were doing. Participating in dialogues and debates about crucial issues was far more effective for the students' learning than sitting down to hear lectures about those issues. Young people in our debate program were making good choices about their health, and they were staying in school. Many of them were at the top of their classes, and all of them had plans to further their education.

At the time, DED used to give small grants of around 3,000 to 5,000 US Dollars, and was happy to donate to our work. It was a big boost to an organization just starting to manage small funds, and it was enough to make an impact. With that funding from DED, we were able to extend into the rural areas of Rwanda. We went into Rulindo District, which is well known for its passion fruit and tea plantations, and, with the help of the mayor and local authorities, organized debates with youth from the community and about twelve schools.

During the activities, those young people in Rulindo, like their counterparts in Kigali, voiced their desire for programs that would help them support themselves.

"Now I know what you want, so prepare yourself," I told them confidently. "I'm going to talk to the donors and I'll be back soon so we can get started."

Big mistake.

I thought getting funding would be easy, especially since I was not going to repeat the mutual fund model and hand out microloans. But to my surprise, neither DED nor any other potential donor believed I was the right person to implement the project. At the time, I was frustrated with the rejection of my proposal. Why couldn't they understand that such an initiative would change people's lives? In hindsight, they were right to be concerned because I was asking for a substantial amount of money, and I had no successful example of having helped people create sustainable livelihoods.

When I told Aline about my failure to raise funds I had promised, she urged me to go back and tell the people in Rulindo that it didn't work out. I organized another meeting with the local authorities and the would-be beneficiaries. I was honest and told them I had sincerely hoped to implement, but there was no funding because of my lack of experience. They had thought their financial situation and living standards were about to change, and I could see the disappointment on their faces.

"At least you have come back," the community leader said, graciously. "Some people come, invoke our interest, raise our hopes, and then when they go they never come back. We are thankful that at least you have come back to us to say it didn't work out."

Soon, with the good audits and excellent reports on how we were managing the small funds from DED, I felt ready and more qualified to reach out to other big donors. Many of them became interested because they were moved by our commitment and the large-scale impact, all accomplished with a small level of funding. That's how I came to engage with Plan International, a development and humanitarian organization that promotes children's rights and equality for girls in over 70 countries around the globe. They began operating in Rwanda in 2007, and by the time I approached them, they knew I existed and was already doing something. PAJER finally had a profile.

Within two years of their arrival in Rwanda, I signed an agreement with Plan International and the dream of an economic empowerment program finally became reality when they gave us funds to rehabilitate a youth center, and to implement the SAFI microfinance program. Both activities were in Gatsibo District, Eastern Province.

The youth center was housed in a small, old building in the Kiramuruzi sector. We rehabilitated it and brought in close to a hundred young people who were finishing secondary school, or had already graduated and wanted to gain skills that would help them in the workforce. We gave them career guidance, trained them in basic computer skills, and taught them how to write a CV and how to interview for a job. We also set up a debate program, taught media skills such as video production, and organized sporting activities such as volleyball and football.

One young woman who came to the center was enthusiastic about all the courses except Computer Skills. Beatrice had been out of school for some time and was afraid to even sit down at the computer because she didn't know how to turn it on. She told us she used to make excuses whenever she was offered a job that required the use of a computer. With some encouragement from our trainers, Beatrice finally agreed to sign up for the class. After the first few days we noticed she was always the first to arrive, practicing before the instructor even started. When the training ended, her confidence level had gone way up and the first thing she did was add computer skills to her CV.

The microfinance program also had a good start. SAFI stands for Sustainable Access to Financial Services for Investment, and the savings and loans program we implemented with Plan International was intended for the poorest people in the communities. The idea was that they would form groups, which we called Voluntary Savings and Loans Associations (VSLAs), then members would carry out income-generating activities, save money within the group's coffers, and eventually be able to take out loans. The funding we got from Plan International was to cover training for six hundred beneficiaries—all young women and men between the ages of 18 and 24.

We decided to work within the limits of the SAFI project's main donor, but to be so innovative and efficient that we would accomplish a lot more than what was realistic for the funds received. In order to make the program reach more people than we were supposed to help, we needed to recruit volunteers from within the community who would help set up extra groups of beneficiaries. The funds we had received covered cash boxes, member pass books, registers, ink pads, and calculators for the identified beneficiaries. We were unable to provide these materials for the extra participants, and our staff and volunteers would have to encourage them to invest in those materials before investing in their small businesses.

We wondered if it was going to work. In most countries it's commonplace and expected that you invest in your personal and professional development, but in much of Africa—at least where we were at the time—it was unheard of to tell a poor person looking to you for help, "I'm going to provide training for you, but you need to get the materials yourself." Another reason we thought people might not willingly support their own training was the distance they would have to walk to get to the bank with their deposits: 10-20 kilometers, or 6-12 miles, carrying cash. In the end, we felt that if they were given a message of hope—that investing in themselves today would help them be better off tomorrow—it would work.

But there was a huge obstacle that we did not expect: resistance from the would-be beneficiaries. What we kept hearing was, "You NGOs, you come, you tell us what to do, we do it, and then you move out and we go back to ground zero. We don't trust you."

We had to spend a good bit of time mobilizing and talking to people to convince them that we were different, that ours was a new approach, and that the program was eventually going to be run by them.

When the the people finally came on board, the first thing we did was identify the six hundred official beneficiaries, and select the volunteers who would reach out to others beyond that number. We explained to the volunteers that we were trying to stretch the limited resources that we had, so more than six hundred people could benefit from the savings and loans program. A feat like that requires a lot of hard work and commitment by the staff on the ground, and it takes extraordinary passion.

The volunteers showed up daily, and tried to coax people in their own neighborhoods to join the program.

But there were more obstacles.

First, all the would-be beneficiaries were hesitant to be placed into the large groups of 40-50 which we were trying to form, and they had justifiable reasons.

"If I'm the 40th person in line, when will I ever get that money?" they wanted to know.

We had not thought about how the rotational nature of the loans would affect them. We also hadn't thought about how much time they could afford to spend on attending the entrepreneurship training we had planned.

"You're not paying us, so we can't afford to spend a half day or more learning how to run a business and how to save money," they said. "We need to work."

We understood their concerns and adjusted our program so that training fit into the two hours they said they could spare, and group-size was reduced to the 20-25 that they recommended. We had not done a baseline survey or consulted them before we went in with our proposal, and that was a big mistake. We learned a valuable lesson and revised our strategies based on what the people wanted. That's a lesson we continue to apply to whatever we do today.

Once we changed our plans to meet the real needs, the energy in the SAFI program became like a massive fire spreading in a dry desert, and the original beneficiary list of six hundred developed into thousands as the volunteers worked with our staff to set up groups. The groups even decided to pay the volunteers a little money to make sure that they continued their supporting role. It was an amazing experience for all involved, and one of the most rewarding experiences we ever had as an organization.

Unlike the failed mutual fund experience, microfinance was a great success with this program because Plan International had introduced us to the Grameen Bank's model of microcredit. Grameen Bank and its founder, Muhammad Yunus, won the Nobel Prize in 2006 for pioneering the concept of microcredit and microfinance to help the poor. The idea is to give small loans with reasonable payback terms, and no collateral required. We tailored this basic concept to our own environment, and it worked much better than giving people "free money" because they now had a personal investment in the scheme.

———

After our partnership with Plan International began, many other opportunities came along. One of them was a Water, Sanitation and Hygiene (WASH) project at the district level, which was sponsored by UNICEF—the United Nations Children's Fund. PAJER worked with health officers in several districts in the Northern Province to develop educational programs, hygiene kits, and posters with messages about hand-washing and other health concerns.

Wherever we went, we kept up our flagship debate program with students and out-of-school youth, teaching them the importance and the mechanics of sharing their opinions and supporting arguments peacefully. Alongside the debates, we extended to more and more youth centers with vocational training, cultural activities, and sexual health education. We also continued to set up Village Savings and Loans Associations.

As an organization, we work with large groups of people, but within each group there are always some who excel and exemplify the transformation and success we want them all to achieve. One such person was a young man who we met on the streets of Musanze doing nothing. Joseph was the oldest in a family of six and had dropped out of school. We put him into a savings and loans program with us, and when the initial three-month training ended, he asked for help to start a shoe repair shop.

We paid a professional shoemaker to teach Joseph how to repair shoes, and as soon as he was eligible, Joseph borrowed funds from his group to buy materials and tools, and to rent a tiny space for his shop. The space was only about one metre by one and a half metres. Less than five square feet. Then he made himself some shelves and wrote on a piece of timber in Kinyarwanda, *Hano Dusana Inkweto*, which means *We repair shoes here*.

We were shocked by the community response to this new business. Most people couldn't afford to buy new shoes, so everyone had shoes to repair! As the project continued during the course of the year, we would visit Joseph and find him busy working, and all the shelves full of shoes and sandals. He was earning a minimum of 20,000 Rwf per week with his business, and was able to help his parents support all his younger siblings. He was even able to hire an assistant to help him with the work.

Another person who stands out in my mind is a woman named Marie-Claire. She didn't say much at the monthly VSLA meetings, but steadily contributed to the group's savings even though she could hardly afford to buy food or clothes. When she got her first loan, she invested in farming beans. After three months she sold the harvest, paid back the loan, and bought metal roofing sheets. With a second loan, she went into maize farming, which she knew would bring in more money. Marie-Claire bought more building materials with money from the maize harvest, and after three or four loan cycles, was able to build a house of her own. Her success boosted her confidence tremendously, and the other group members appointed her group secretary.

Our microfinance program was changing the lives of thousands like Marie-Claire, Joseph, and their families.

At the beginning, PAJER was standing on one leg, and then with the help received from Plan International and others, we had two legs firmly on the ground. Prayers had been answered and there was balance now: we had the debates, we had support for some of the critical issues that young people were discussing during the course of the debate program, and we had a number of partners helping us branch out into new areas of service on behalf of the youth and the poor. I was grateful for the support and the progress, and finally felt I was being the resourceful person my parents had wanted me to be.

9

NEW DIRECTION

I resigned from a well-paying job to start an organization dedicated to working with people affected by poverty and conflict, and, six years later, after a difficult beginning, PAJER had grown in both personnel and programs. We moved from having a team of five staff including myself, to ten, and then fifteen. Donor agencies and some generous individuals funded our programs, and our plan for the future was simply to expand the debate, vocational training, and microfinance programs to more districts within Rwanda.

Then, one day in 2012, I turned on the television at home and saw images of an influx of refugees streaming into Rwanda. Over twenty-five thousand men, women, and children were fleeing the fighting between rebels and the government in the eastern part of the DR Congo. The news footage of displaced families and refugee children captivated me.

Though I was busy and happy supporting youth and the Rwandan community through debate and economic empowerment programs, I prayed that God would bless me with an opportunity to support the refugees too. After my experience growing up in exile, I felt I could do something to help them.

I didn't know exactly how I would help the refugees, but when it came to refugee life, what I did know was this: In refugee settings most parents are desperate because of the nature of the life they are living, and they tend not to have time to give adequate attention to their children. They simply struggle to survive from day to day, and food, medicine and shelter are priorities. Children can lose vision and focus, and sometimes also lose hope despite outside efforts to give them comfort and psychological support. It's never easy, as no matter how welcoming the host, refugees can never replicate the good life they lived in their country of origin, or forget the trauma that caused them to leave.

Many refugee children have been affected by the violence they have seen, and some have lost siblings or parents. It doesn't matter where they have come from, or why they have fled. All that matters is that they need someone on their side—someone to lessen the pain of the disparities that they will surely feel.

As I looked at images of the influx, I knew I didn't want to see these refugee children ruin their lives by taking drugs, like so many of the young refugees I knew in Uganda. I didn't want to see them sitting idle and not going to school when they have the right to do so. I had parents who managed to make time to nurture me beyond providing basic needs, and so I wanted to see these children studying hard, getting the best we could give them, and being able to imagine a better future despite the difficulties. I wanted to be part of the Emergency Response Team, and I wanted to help the children by improving the day-to-day lives of their parents. I knew that would make me even happier and more fulfilled than I already was.

A short while after the influx began, I went to the United Nations High Commissioner for Refugees (UNHCR) to see if there was a role PAJER could play.

When I arrived at the gate, I told the security guard I wanted to meet the person in charge of supporting local partners.

"What's the person's name?" the guard asked.

I didn't have an answer, and tried to find out from him who that person was.

"I'm sorry," he said. "We are not allowed to do that. If you don't have an appointment, we can't let you in."

I went home feeling hopeless, wondering how I would ever know the men and women who were in that building.

In the following days I made several other attempts to contact someone at UNHCR, but all doors were closed to me. Then one day, many weeks after my first attempt, I happened to see a program about the Ministry of Disaster Preparedness and Refugee Affairs (Now known as the Ministry of Disaster Management and Refugee Affairs [MIDIMAR]) on television. It was a relatively new ministry, and the program was about their role and how they worked with UN agencies and other partners. I learned that before any organization could even start operating in Rwanda as a partner, the government had to approve them. I decided I would go and talk to the Permanent Secretary of the Ministry of Refugee Affairs to see if he could help me, and the very next morning, I went to the Ministry and knocked on his door.

Antoine Ruvebana had been appointed Permanent Secretary in May of 2011, a year before the influx. I managed to see him but he told me he was on his way to a meeting, and asked if I could come back the next day. His secretary set up an appointment, and the next day I went back and had a proper meeting with him. We discovered one thing we both had in common was a degree in Education from a Rwandan university, followed by a one-year teaching position before we moved into what we truly wanted for our lives. I told him more about my personal background and my work experience, and shared my thoughts about the Congolese refugee situation.

"Patrick, we don't give funding, but don't worry," the Permanent Secretary told me. "We have a Refugee Coordination Meeting next week and I would like to invite you to be part of it so you can meet all the players. There is a lot of work to do, and we need people to support us."

That kind of encouragement was something I didn't expect, and although I knew God had big plans for me, I wouldn't have imagined this. I couldn't hide my emotions, and I think my visible relief and appreciation gave him the impression that I truly had passion for my work and for what I wanted to do.

When I went back a week later for the meeting at the Ministry of Refugee Affairs, networking was my top priority. I knew I would be given the opportunity to talk about myself, and I hoped that by the time I left the meeting I would have gained some contacts that would lead to future work and opportunities to serve.

In that room was the top leadership of the UN agencies, as well as representatives from several international NGOs such as Oxfam and the American Refugee Committee. PAJER had been invited by the government to be a part of the meeting so that we could introduce our work and ask for a chance to offer support to the Refugee sector and the Emergency Response Team. When I sat with all of them, including Neimah Warsame, the representative of UNHCR, I knew this was the biggest opportunity I would ever have.

Most of the humanitarian sectors were represented at the Refugee Coordination Meeting. Among them were Health, Protection, Shelter, and WASH (Water, Sanitation and Hygiene). All of them had a role to play in the intervention to the refugee crisis, but there was one gap: No one had signed up for Food Security, which mostly would involve distribution of food and non-food items. When this need was discussed, I raised my hand and volunteered.

"We don't have money in the budget for food distribution," Madame Warsame told me, apologetically.

Then Permanent Secretary Ruvebana stepped in. "I know this man is new, and you don't have money," he said, "but he has the capacity in terms of energy, and he has a team. According to what he has told me, I know he will serve the refugees with dignity and passion."

Someone else spoke up and repeated, "We don't have money."

I replied, "I don't want money, I want to support the people."

"Why would you support people without money?" they asked, looking at me like I was out of my mind.

"I've been reading a lot about the emergency response and what you need," I said, looking at the faces around the room. "You're talking about food supply. You're talking about distribution of food in the camps, and you say you need a partner. I can distribute food with my team. It doesn't require a lot of money to do that. Give me a chance. Trust me, and you won't be disappointed."

The PS spoke up for me again, this time more vehemently, and told them, "This guy has said that he can do it. Why don't you give him a chance? Give him a chance!"

I remained quiet and waited. My mind went back to my life in Uganda, and I thought about how, in that environment, refugees were often considered liabilities rather than assets, and non-citizens with no rights and nothing to contribute. God had been good to my family, and I wanted to help refugees who were suffering far more and would want to be treated with dignity and respect.

I looked around at the people sitting at the table with me. I suspected they were reluctant to say yes because most UN agencies had no confidence in local organizations and thought we were not up to the task. In the humanitarian and development field there are still myths and stereotypes about what Africans and African organizations can and cannot do.

When someone finally spoke up, it was to question my capacity.

"It's not rocket science," I answered. "Getting food to the people is not something that needs capacity. It needs the will and the heart. A big heart. It's as simple as that."

The Permanent Secretary, who was chairing the meeting on behalf of the government, spoke up yet again, more gently this time. "Give them a chance," he said. "Patrick has told me how hard-working his team is. There are not enough Rwandans or other Africans doing the kind of work PAJER is doing."

I'm sorry to say, but even after that encouragement from the PS, some people in the room were still wary and couldn't understand why I was interested in taking on the food distribution. Nevertheless, that meeting with the Permanent Secretary and the donor agencies was a big turning point for PAJER. By the end of it, I had an appointment to talk to a staff member at UNHCR to see if my willingness to work in food distribution, despite the limitations, would be something they could exploit.

Now that I was invited to the UNHCR offices, the security guard gave me access when I showed up at the gate, and I went in to meet with a senior program officer.

Fred was an African national who welcomed me with a smile and an enthusiastic handshake, and told me right away that he was happy to see a local initiative joining the humanitarian effort.

"We are going to prepare a contract that gives you access to the Kigeme Refugee Camp," he said, "but it is a zero budget agreement."

When I asked him if he had ever prepared such an agreement before, he said I was the first person who had ever volunteered to do such a thing.

"Are you sure you want to do this?" he asked.

I said, "Yes, I'm ready to go. Should I fail, I'll come back to you and say 'I'm sorry, but I have done my best and I have failed,' but I don't think that will happen."

Fred wished me luck and reminded me that our results would affect every other local organization coming after us. But I already knew that.

Many of the other NGOs on the Emergency Response Team thought it would be impossible for PAJER to manage on a zero budget even for a day. How does any ordinary person keep their staff for free? Distribution of food required teams of people and a reliable vehicle. I had no car. I had nothing. There was nothing in my life that had been easy, but I was driven by passion. I said to myself, *Even if I distribute food for two days, I'll be a happy man; I'll have done something and made a difference.* And so I signed the contract for zero funds. Not even a *per diem* for anyone. Not even 1,000 Rwandan francs, or $2 a day, for food. Zero.

I went to Permanent Secretary Ruvebana to update him on the situation, and he was sympathetic, telling me he wished he had the means to do more. I thanked him for all he had already done, and then I prayed, *Oh God, you've given me the opportunity, but you've also given me a challenge.*

Next, I went to talk to my team. Many of the individuals were young men and women I had employed to work with PAJER on a youth arts and media training project funded by Plan International, and our work together had recently ended. They had all been hoping UNHCR would give us a chance to work with the refugees so I could keep them on. That day, I told them the whole story and explained clearly that there would be a lot of work, but no pay.

"Who's ready to move all the way with me in this darkness?" I asked. "I have nothing to offer you except personal satisfaction for a job that will be well done."

All of them took some time to weigh their options. They were excited about the opportunity to work and do something good, but they had to think about survival too. Some of them had family to feed.

"Don't feel obligated to say yes," I told them, "but trust that He who provided the opportunity will provide the means. Do your part, and God will do his part."

Understandably, most of them were not ready to make the sacrifice, and by the end of the evening, only four gentlemen had committed to implementing the food distribution for free. One of them was Dominic Kagenza, a down-to-earth Christian who I had known for a long time even outside my work with PAJER. He was a hard worker and I knew his maturity and his calm, simple manner would be good for the team. I put him in charge of the other three enthusiastic volunteers, and in charge of the whole operation. Together, we all started preparing to take that leap of faith.

The day after my small staff agreed to work with me for zero funds, I was walking to the PAJER office when an old friend saw me and pulled over in his SUV. I had met Canisius when I first returned to Rwanda, and we hadn't seen each other for years. I didn't recognize him right away, because he had gained some weight.

"It's me, Canisius!" he shouted, leaning out of the window to wave me over. "Why are you walking? Don't you have a car?"

"Canisius, life has been good to you!" I said. The last time I had seen him, he was importing cars from Dubai, so I added, jokingly, "I need a vehicle. Maybe you could give me one!"

"Patrick, there is nothing that I can't give you," he said. "Take a car and pay me when you have money, even if it's ten years from now."

I stood there speechless. Although I had been receiving funding for PAJER's various programs, my salary was only a small fraction of each budget, and I had no disposable income. Some projects were short-term, and it was tough to make ends meet. I felt like I was in a dream. Then I heard Canisius say, "Get into the car. I have cars that are still in customs, and you can pick the one you want. Let's go now. I don't want to see you walking anymore."

God, what is this? I asked silently, as I climbed into his vehicle. *What is happening?*

We drove to MAGERWA, Rwanda's cargo handling facility, and I picked a silver Toyota RAV4. It was my first good car, and Canisius paid the taxes so I got it with no money down. This happened the week before we had to start the distribution of food.

The team was excited about PAJER's new venture, but I was a bit concerned. I had set aside enough money to fuel the car for the three and a half hour drive to Kigeme Refugee Camp, and had only 50,000 Rwf left for minimal living expenses. Dominic and I had to figure out how we would manage with 50,000 Rwf between the five of us, and nothing else coming in.

As the departure date approached we went about our preparations, and if the volunteers were worried, they kept it to themselves. As usual, I had one or two grant proposals out, and prayed silently that something would come through. We had been waiting a long time for a yes or a no from one potential donor, and I found myself spending quite a bit of time checking my email to see if there was a response. Just before we were due to leave, there it was! I had to double-check to believe it. ICCO, a Dutch development organization, had come through with funds for our conflict management and economic empowerment programs, and we were able to allocate some of those funds to support us at the camp with housing and small allowances for food.

Preparations for the trip turned even more joyful, and we began to look for a place to stay. Dominic managed to rent a small house near the camp from a kind man who was willing to trust our word that the money was coming soon, and everyone agreed they would live there together, making do with a couple of mattresses on the floor. How could we have gone to the field and done the work without these miracles of a vehicle and a house? We were doing our part, and God, who is always faithful, was doing his.

The Kigeme Refugee Camp is built on and around two large hills in Nyamagabe District, in Rwanda's Southern Province. The Southern Province is also home to Huye District, where my father was born, and Nyanza District, where my grandfather worked as a supervisor on coffee farms of the Belgians.

As we drove through Nyanza and then Butare, the capital city of Huye, I couldn't help thinking of my father and wishing he could see the progress Rwanda had made as a nation, and the way our family had grown. Most of my siblings were married with children, and Aline and I were now the parents of a boy and two girls who inspired us to strive for the best we could offer to them, and to the nation where they were growing up.

As we finally approached the camp, all of us in the vehicle became quiet. The two hills before us in the distance, known as Site A and Site B, were dotted with white UNHCR tents and many of the men, women, and children who used those tents as shelters. There were eighteen thousand refugees at Kigeme, and our small team had to feed all of them on a regular basis. How were we going to do it? Would our collective will and our big hearts truly be enough?

When we started the distribution of food we could see people losing patience. So often we would find someone crying because he needed food, but his turn to get food was in two days' time, or even more. There was a distribution order we needed to follow, and certain things we needed to take into consideration, like family size and vulnerability levels. But dealing with people who were hungry, while trying to follow the proper procedures, was a difficult situation for us. The mothers with children were an especially vulnerable group, and they made our emotions run high. We were conflicted.

It was hard to hear the cries and not do anything about it, so we turned to the refugees themselves for help. We learned from them that with the system the way it was, with food distribution taking two full weeks to cover the entire camp, people ran out of food long before they were able to get their new rations. My team and I studied the food distribution manuals and asked ourselves how we could do better.

After some brainstorming and strategizing, we decided to work with individuals from the refugee community as partners. With more workers on board, we could create more teams, offload the food trucks faster, and increase the number of distribution points. We asked UNHCR to provide payment for the casual laborers from the refugee community, and they agreed. We also called for more help from the PAJER office, and got two more of our staff members, another man and a young woman named Esperance, to join us in the field.

When our larger team was in place, we increased the number of hours for distribution. We began work at six o'clock in the morning instead of at the customary eight-thirty. Each day, instead of waiting for the World Food Programme truck to bring in the new rations, we started with what was still left in the storeroom. By the time the trucks arrived at eight o'clock, we were already actively in the process, so no time was wasted. Finally, we worked up until six in the evening, where in normal circumstances food distribution stopped around four-thirty.

Basically, because we wanted different results, we did everything differently. Within a month of taking over the food distribution at Kigeme Refugee Camp, our strategy had reduced the distribution time from two weeks to three days. This struck UNHCR like a bolt of lightning. They couldn't believe it, and wanted to know how it was done. They requested detailed reports, which added to the work my core team was already doing. Dominic put Esperance in charge of coordinating the paperwork, which meant she had to deliver forms to all the distribution sites, and collect the records from them at the end of each day.

The team would leave the distribution centers in the evening, often having worked without a break, and sit down to compile a report about how many hundreds of metric tons of food were distributed that day. They worked on the reports all evening and would go to bed after midnight. By 5 A.M. they were up with the roosters and getting ready to go out in the camp again.

In the beginning of our seventh month of distributing food at Kigeme Refugee Camp, UNHCR Representative Neimah Warsame called while I was in Kigali to say they were extremely happy with the work we were doing so efficiently, despite not having a budget.

"The commitment, vision, and work ethic I'm seeing in this organization are incredible," she said. "Your performance has exceeded our expectations, and I'm going to ask my office to work on the contract so that we can formalize our agreement and pay you from this point forward."

I was ecstatic to hear this, as anyone can imagine. But because of the exceptional results my team had produced, I decided to ask them to compensate us for all of the time we had worked for free. After a face-to-face meeting, the UNHCR Representative agreed. Not only would they now pay our salaries and running costs, but they would compensate us for the seven months we worked without pay. I couldn't wait to share the news with my team at Kigeme.

I drove to the camp and found Dominic, Esperance, and the rest of the staff that evening, getting ready for their post-work meeting. When I told them the good news, they wept with joy. The news was a relief and a blessing for all of us.

"This is what I was talking about months ago when this opportunity came up," I said. "You did what you thought was right in the eyes of the Lord, and God did his part."

In one week's time the contract was signed, and UNHCR paid us all the money, seven months almost, making us a fully funded implementing partner. We continued to work with even more energy than before, and even found time to do some work for UNICEF at the camp. They asked PAJER to come up with a proposal to support young people, who made up over sixty percent of the refugees, and needed something to do. Among other things, we established a small library in a tent, created a reproductive health program, and did some training in basic hygiene and sanitation.

Our activities at the camp kept us very busy, and we were thrilled to be making a difference, and to be compensated for our work. We never once imagined that our circumstances would soon change again.

Not long after we signed the new contract with UNHCR, the organization in charge of WASH at Kigeme left the camp without notice. UNHCR was desperate to find an organization to fill in the gap, and a program officer within the agency suggested us.

I got the call one afternoon when I was on my way to pick my son up from school. It was the head of UNHCR, asking me if PAJER had any experience with water, sanitation and hygiene. I told her about the WASH project I had done with UNICEF a year or so earlier, and assured her that we could fill in the gap at Kigeme if given the opportunity. God had shown me every single step up to this point in my life, so I knew we wouldn't fail here after succeeding in other difficult circumstances.

When I went to UNHCR to start discussions, they told me there was no time to waste because there was a disease outbreak in the camp. They signed us up as a partner on the spot and transferred the funds immediately. Everything was happening at the same time—the reimbursement for our seven months of unpaid work, followed by this opportunity to play another major role in the Emergency Response. It was like a rainstorm after a drought. In a few months we stabilized the outbreak, put the camp back on track, and had visitors who noticed the remarkable improvement at the camp and praised us publicly.

With our new role at the camp, **PAJER** became part of a network of humanitarian organizations working in Rwanda. Water, Sanitation and Hygiene was our focus, but while we had had some experience, we clearly needed more training if we were to make it one of the strongest pillars of our organization.

When thousands of displaced people are pouring in to a neighboring country to search for refuge, how do you make sure you have enough WASH facilities? A large influx is a volatile situation and can cause outbreaks of cholera and other diseases. How do you respond to such an influx? We had no answers because we had never been faced with that situation before, so we began to participate in sector working groups where members exchange information, share valuable experience and innovations, and learn from each other. **UNHCR** happened to have the best technical expertise in **WASH** so we worked with their experts to set up and complete training modules for our staff and volunteers.

The work at Kigeme Refugee Camp was the turning point in our intentions, leading **PAJER** into the humanitarian field, and giving our lives new meaning and purpose.

PHOTOGRAPHS

"Pure water is the source of life."
One of our WASH projects at Kigeme Refugee Camp.

Voluntary Savings and Loans Associations (VSLAs) meet regularly to deposit savings and take out or pay back loans.

Me with sponsors and winners of the 2016 Rwanda Speaks debate competition. Giving young people a platform to express their views is an important component of GHDF's Youth Empowerment Program.

Trainees in the tailoring program at the Peak Family Itorero Youth Center

Health ambassadors rally students for HIV Voluntary Counseling and Testing at Nkomero School in Nyanza District.

GHDF staff and partners have reached almost 200,000 adolescents with programs designed to prevent HIV and eliminate stigma for those living with the virus.

Refugee leaders speak up at a camp event.

Carrying on cultural traditions and activities is an important part of life for Burundians at Mahama Refugee Camp.

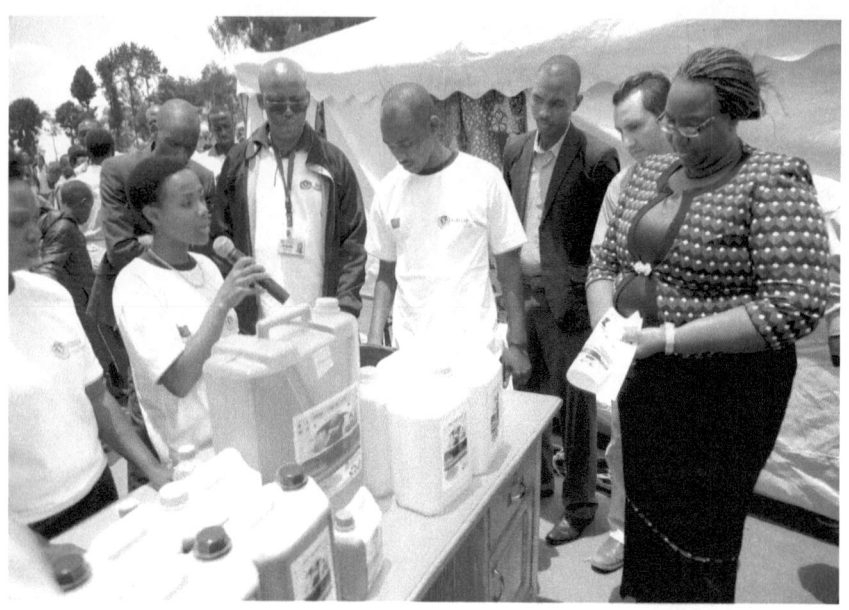

Beneficiaries of the US State Department's Julia Taft Fund for Refugees show off the soap and clothing they produced in the vocational training program at Kigeme Refugee Camp. Graduates formed VSLAs and started small businesses.

Refugees appreciate being hired to help improve their living conditions.

GHDF designed a new latrine for improved sanitation.

Trainers show visitors a "Talking Book" developed by Literacy Bridge, and used to deliver health and hygiene messages to camp residents.

At the Mahama Camp with UNHCR Representative Ahmed Baba Fall.

Global Humanitarian and Development Foundation has programs in all of Rwanda's provinces.

With GHDF staff at the Kigali office.

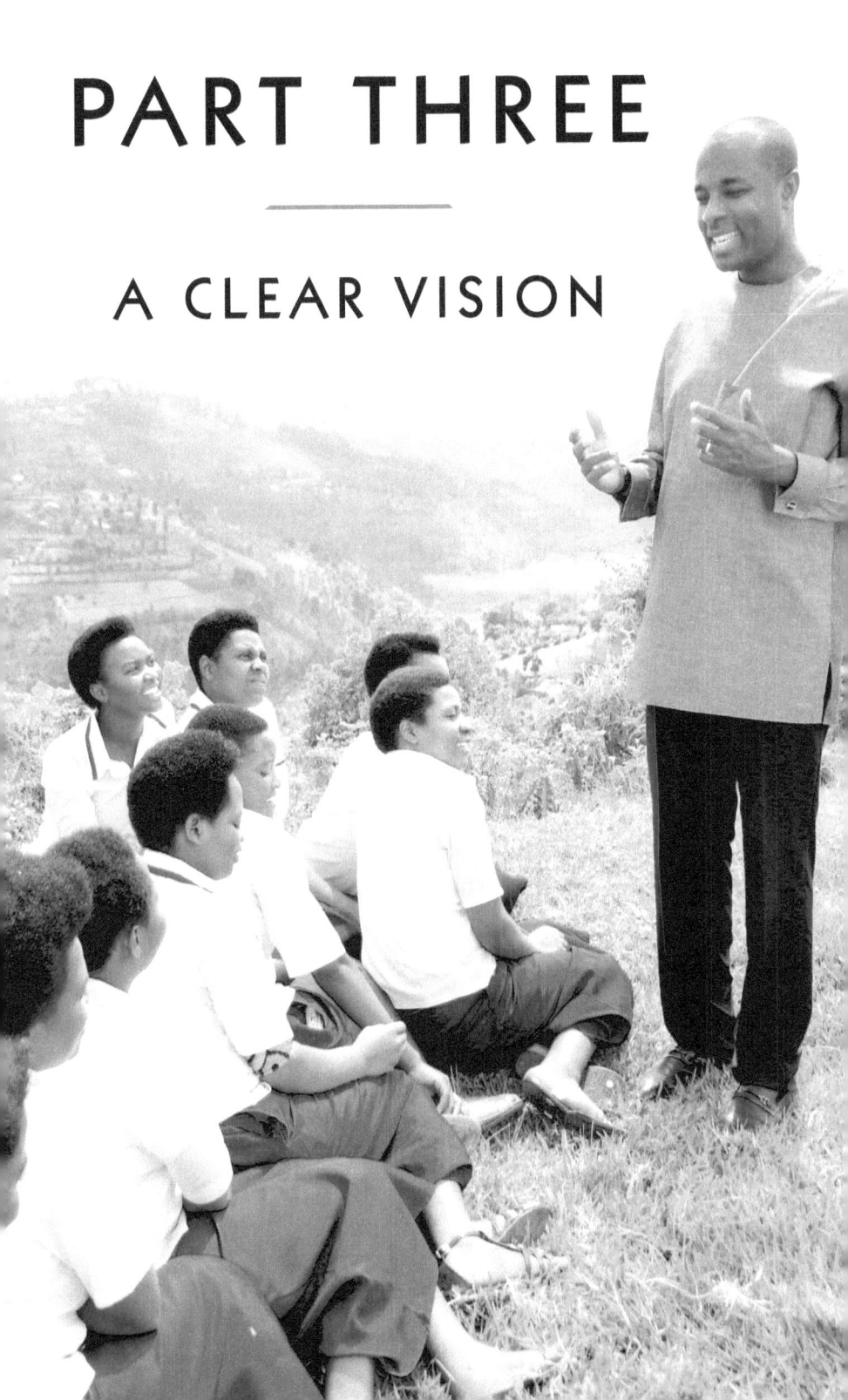

PART THREE

A CLEAR VISION

10

A GLOBAL REACH BEGINS AT HOME

"The size of your dreams must always exceed your current capacity to achieve them. If your dreams do not scare you, they are not big enough."

—President Ellen Johnson Sirleaf

With PAJER taking on much bigger responsibilities after we became an implementing partner for UNHCR, I decided it was time to revisit the hope I once had to study economics and business management. I enrolled in an Executive MBA program at Mount Kenya University's campus in Rwanda because I wanted to gain new skills and insight into different managerial and leadership approaches. I also wanted to improve on strategic thinking, and develop better communication and team-building skills. I was starting to think of reaching beyond

Rwanda's borders, and knew that being in such a program could help me understand what it would take to do so. It was especially nice to have my wife join me in this undertaking, as she was quite involved in PAJER's work as well.

I continued working full-time while studying, and around this time became an implementing partner in a large project dedicated to, and named, *Building an Inclusive Financial Sector in Rwanda*. BIFSIR was set within the framework of Rwanda's National Microfinance Strategy, and funded by the United Nations Development Programme (UNDP), the United Nations Capital Development Fund (UNCDF), One UN Fund, the Republic of Korea, and the Government of Rwanda. This initiative enabled us to set up even more Voluntary Savings and Loans Associations across the country.

By the end of 2015, PAJER had over twenty-three thousand people in almost eight hundred VSLAs. That year, PAJER also received funding from the US State Department's Julia Taft Fund for Refugees for a pilot project that allowed us to bring the SAFI microfinance program to refugees for the first time. It was a one-year project to train just over a hundred refugees at the Kigeme Camp in Information and Communications Technology (ICT), tailoring, tie-dyeing, and basic financial education. After the training, which included business development and VSL methodology, the beneficiaries formed themselves into four Associations and set up their own small cooperatives and individual businesses.

Although the training opportunity was only given to a small fraction of people in need, it was a good way to test our model for facilitating sustainable livelihoods within the refugee population. Some outstanding examples of success include Solange Muraza, a woman who fled from the DRC with her family, leaving behind a good living as a farmer. At Kigeme she was trained in tailoring, and was able to buy her own sewing machine when the training ended. She now produces clothes, handbags, school uniforms, and other items, and her new skills earn her enough money to be able to send all her children to school.

Another farmer from the DRC, Faustin Ndabarinze, was trained in ICT and dreamed of opening a cyber café with other graduates from the program. On graduation day he was confident that they could use their new skills to meet a real need for fellow refugees and for local Rwandans who live near the camp.

One more story I want to share is that of Nadia Mukede, who escaped from the Congo to avoid being raped by fighters. She and her younger brother ran away together, leaving behind their parents. The transition was difficult, but her brother goes to school now, and Nadia makes beautiful tie-dyed tablecloths that she sells to support them both.

The best part of the Julia Taft Fund project was that it gave the refugees confidence and hope. The people who benefitted from it had new income-generating skills and were no longer sitting around waiting for food rations at the end of the month. A small group of refugees had launched into livelihoods on a small scale successfully, and surveys and observations a few months after their training showed that many of them were still working enthusiastically. We know that with major support, the same activities can be implemented even more effectively in other camps as well.

Over the years, **PAJER** grew where we expected it, but beyond our expectations at the same time. We received increasingly higher levels of support and steadily expanded our programs. Our reach soon became wide enough to warrant a name change that would better reflect what we do, and what we hope to do in the future. Calling ourselves Rwanda Youth Parliament was no longer accurate because we had expanded our work far beyond debating the critical issues of the day, and so in 2016, **PAJER** officially became the Global Humanitarian and Development Foundation (GHDF).

At GHDF we currently have four main programs, the largest of which is the Humanitarian Response Program that supports almost one hundred thousand refugees and people in need. We have extended our humanitarian response services to the Mahama Refugee Camp in response to an influx of refugees fleeing violence and insecurity in Burundi, and we now work in three different reception centers where newly arriving refugees are sheltered until the camps are ready to receive them.

Located in the Eastern Province, Mahama is a huge camp that now hosts around sixty thousand refugees, divided into several "villages". When Mahama was first opened, there were some challenges with sanitation and shelters. Keeping the pit latrines clean was a major problem because large numbers of people had to share them. At the time, large groups of refugees lived in hangars until they could be moved to tents, and the close proximity in those hangars also caused some hygiene issues.

As partners in water, sanitation, and hygiene, GHDF first took on the construction of sanitation facilities at the Mahama Refugee Camp. We designed a latrine with a special toilet pan that keeps odor out, and does not allow flies to come in and sit on feces. The toilet pan prevents the spread of pathogens, and is easy for anyone, even children and people living with disabilities, to use. The new latrines are assigned to small groups of families who are responsible for cleaning them, and we don't have to dislodge, or empty them, until they have been in use for three years or so. We constructed over five hundred blocks of easily dischargeable latrines, with one block serving only four families.

As the latrines were being built, we also constructed shelters to replace the hangars and tents. One of the Mahama village chiefs, Fulgence Nkeraguhiga, remembers spending a lot of time taking his children to the hospital when they lived in a hangar, because they were always affected by coughs, flu, pneumonia, and infections caused by poor hygiene. He says the new shelters give his family space and privacy, keep them healthy, protect them during the rainy season, and moderate the heat of the sun during the dry season.

We have been facilitating access to potable water, constructing and maintaining shelters and sanitation facilities, conducting hygiene promotion campaigns, and managing waste in two refugee camps—Kigeme and Mahama—and three reception centers. Without access to such services, the danger of diarrhea, cholera, typhoid and other disease outbreaks would be high.

In the three reception centers, we truck in enough water to provide each person with 20 liters per day. In partnership with UNHCR, we have built a water treatment plant at the Bugesera reception center, eliminating the need for trucking in water. This plant also provides clean water to the nearby host community.

One major challenge we faced at Mahama, even after the new latrines were built, was the prevalence of open defecation. Due to cultural beliefs, many refugees were afraid to use the latrines and preferred to defecate out in the bushes and woods. They told us if they used the latrines, their cows back home would die. With the help of UNICEF, we trained over three hundred hygiene promoters, installed hand-washing facilities near the latrines, and reached out to the refugee community with campaigns about the dangers of open defecation, among other things. Through theater, debate, and songs performed outdoors in front of large crowds, we sensitized camp residents about the benefits and the how-to of using the latrines, hand washing, breastfeeding, and keeping water clean and safe.

Our Economic Development Program, which has been supported by Plan International and the US Department of State's Julia Taft Fund, continues to focus mainly on microfinance initiatives and basic financial education for vulnerable Rwandan and refugee communities. The president and founder of the Benerugo Savings Group, an outgoing woman named Verdiane Mukagakwandi, says the low interest loans that members get from the group allow them to pay for their children's school fees and medical care. She also says that since joining the group, all the members are now able to afford electricity and one-third of them have paid for water connection to their households. The Benerugo group makes shoes and bags, but some of its members have also branched out into agribusiness and commercial ventures like shops and bars.

In the Health and Nutrition Program, the GHDF staff, working alongside local and governmental organizations, supports youth and adults living with HIV, and teaches prevention mechanisms, especially for adolescents between the ages of nine and eighteen. UNICEF is our partner in Health and Nutrition, and together we have trained almost five hundred volunteers to sensitize their communities about HIV, Gender-Based Violence, the benefits of male circumcision, and more. We have reached more than one hundred fifty thousand adolescents with messages, and twenty-two thousand have been voluntarily tested for HIV. People who test positive are directly linked to health services for support so they don't continue spreading the virus, and so they can have access to medication, food, and other support that the health centers provide. Our campaigns also work to prevent stigmatization of infected persons within the communities.

We are supporting nutrition programs, screening anemia cases, and directly linking people to service providers like clinics, hospitals and organizations that provide vitamins and food supplements. We also support agriculture for nutrition with our Farmer Field Schools (FFS). Our FFS trainers work with farmers, and they teach agricultural skills to people at home, showing them how to use a small patch of their land to grow and harvest vegetables. We teach people in the village how to do it in a simple way using their own biodegradable materials.

Also falling under Health and Nutrition is the 1,000 Days Program, in which partners have to respond to some of the most critical nutritional diseases within a thousand days. One thousand days is symbolic of the length of time from conception to a child's second birthday, when nutritional health is most important for mother and child. Those nutritional diseases we fight include anemia, wasting, and the stunting that occurs when children don't get a balanced diet. We are responding to the 1,000 Days Program through the Farmer Field Schools because we know when people have a variety of nutrient-rich vegetables, their children can grow and stay healthy. It doesn't require a lot of money to make a big difference, because with only about fifty seeds a family can have enough vegetables for a year.

Finally, we have the Youth Empowerment and Education Program. The original debate program found its home here, and so did vocational training in tailoring, hairdressing, plumbing, carpentry, computer literacy, and software development. For fun, we also offer classes in Rwandan traditional dance, and sports. Most of our training is based at the Peak Family Itorero Youth Center in Nyamagabe District, and the Isangano Youth Center in Gatsibo District. Graduates from the training programs often go on to use their new skills to earn a living providing services to their communities. One example is Emmanuel Nsanzimana, a young man who signed up for our ICT classes just after he graduated from secondary school. He didn't know anything about computers and thought he was too old to learn. Today he is an IREMBO agent, helping people in his sector pay taxes and other bills online through the one-stop portal for e-government services.

There are often projects that cut across the four main programs, and we continuously strengthen or add programs to meet the needs on the ground.

Where others don't believe something can happen, at GHDF we make it happen. But it's not because we have the most brilliant teams or even the most experienced teams. It's because we have committed people, and it's because we listen to our beneficiaries. The word *beneficiary* has been used for a long time to describe someone who is receiving something, but we recognize that our beneficiaries have a lot to offer and that they often grow from beneficiaries into partners. As I speak of beneficiaries in relation to our work, it's mainly to make a distinction between the partners we are empowering, and the partners who collaborate with us or fund our programs. It is the work of our teams, inspired by the input of our beneficiaries, which enables us to find solutions and create innovative and successful interventions.

I liken our offices and field stations to a hospital emergency room where doctors and nurses are always present. The same applies to the work we do. We are the doctors, we are the nurses, and people need our help in terms of life support. When you are responding to such needs you need to have passion for your work, and the highest level of commitment. I sometimes spend more than a month without going to the refugee camps because of the work in Kigali, or because of travels, and my program staff—now over fifty strong—are the ones who step in and take action, while I simply give feedback. GHDF has an amazing team of self-motivated men and women who care deeply for the people they serve. That has made a big difference in our work, in our results, and in our impact.

I always tell potential staff that working at GHDF is not a place to make a lot of money, but a place to serve. If you want to make a lot of money you can go into business, but if you are working with us it's all about helping people in need. We often work long hours without extra pay, especially when there is an emergency. Our salaries do not correspond with the effort we put in, but we believe our existence is much brighter because of the way we impact people's lives.

The issues we address in Rwanda are not contained within its borders. We share common values and common problems with neighboring countries. GHDF has not done everything we want to do at home, but we have touched the lives of those who sought refuge with us, and our vision is to someday work side by side with them as they help to rebuild or develop their own nations. Our big dream now is to go beyond our borders.

Mainly because of the contact we have had with refugees from the East African region, we would like to see how we can offer support to the DRC and Burundi. We already have an office operational in Uganda, which is now the biggest refugee-hosting country in the region with over one million South Sudanese taking refuge there. We hope to also offer support to Sudan and the Central African Republic. Furthermore, we have explored providing integration services overseas for African refugees emigrating to Canada. A help center of sorts would assist them in navigating the job market, managing their money, and overcoming language and cultural barriers. Our goal would be all about confidence building and eliminating some of the failures that lead to depression.

Over the years I've seen there is a natural growth that stems from what we do at the community level. If you touch one life, ten others are touched. Touch a hundred, and they will touch a thousand. Jesus did not reach everyone's home, but he had disciples who helped him. There were only twelve of them, but because of their commitment to spreading the Gospel, the teachings of Jesus are still positively influencing people over two thousand years since his death and resurrection. It's audacious to someday want to be a global presence, especially since we are still building up resources of our own, but nothing is impossible. We must dream big, believe in ourselves, and take the small steps that will help us meet our goal. A dream realized always begins with small steps, and a global reach always begins at home.

Once, on a trip to Switzerland, the immigration officer at the airport looked at my passport and said, "Oh, you come from Rwanda, the Switzerland of Africa! Your country is doing very well." After many years of Africa being taken as a continent which is not serious, full of corruption, and plagued by poor leadership, there is nothing that makes me prouder than being recognized as someone who comes from a serious country and is not coming to beg or to cause trouble, but as a person who is more of an asset than a liability.

I'm proud of Rwanda, and although what I have done may be small, at least I have done something, and will continue doing all I can for my country. The people of Rwanda have a dream—a vision for the Rwanda we want to see by 2020. A lot of our work at Global Humanitarian and Development Foundation correlates with the official plan for the nation, and we work closely with government bodies to do our part in the country's growth and development.

Over the years, I have seen GHDF grow from humble beginnings. I've seen this organization grow from scratch to where we are at this point, and I have never believed more than I do now, that we are fulfilling God's vision. GHDF has supported and empowered hundreds of thousands of people in the poorest communities. Children we have helped have gone back to school, and can not only imagine, but also attain, a better future. But there is still much to overcome, and so much more to be done.

11

CHALLENGES

"Overcoming poverty is not a task of charity, it is an act of justice. Like Slavery and Apartheid, poverty is not natural. It is man-made and it can be overcome and eradicated by the actions of human beings."

—President Nelson Mandela

At GHDF, we face obstacles and challenges all the time. It is the nature of the work. The most common challenge is perhaps a limited access to funds, and another is a limited access to markets. We experience it as an organization, and our beneficiaries experience it as individuals.

As an organization, we're trying to solve some critical issues affecting the men, women, and youth in the communities, but what we're doing is a mere drop in the ocean. Under the Economic Development Program, we are supporting close to fifty thousand beneficiaries, but the gap between what we do and what is needed is huge. The scale of our work has to expand to support the growth needs of the people, and we are always looking for ways to augment the basic support and training we offer.

GHDF's pilot programs in livelihoods have been successful, but only to a certain extent. Most of the individuals whose stories I have shared belong to Village Savings and Loans Associations, which are made up mostly of vulnerable Rwandans and partly of refugees from DRC and Burundi. They start with a little capacity in terms of capital, but as their businesses grow, those who are ambitious and want to expand may need to be able to borrow larger amounts of money than what the group members have saved. They need access to capital, access to banks, and linkages with financial institutions. But as individuals in the VSLAs do better and better, many of them soon reach a plateau because of limited access to funds, markets, and supporters.

One challenge is that short-term projects can only get them so far. Donors may give money for skills and business training, but if they don't extend that funding or commit to long-term programs from the beginning, it's sometimes difficult for the beneficiaries to put into practice what they've learned, or to scale up their businesses.

Another challenge is that banks are reluctant to lower interest rates. If a VSLA is performing well, it is possible for the group to acquire a big loan. When their small businesses start doing well, we open up the possibility by asking them to open accounts in commercial banks. We train them to periodically save and withdraw, because transactions show that you are making business everyday, and help you win the trust of the bank. We even bring in credit managers to give them an inside look at how the banks work. Some of our groups have already received large loans from financial institutions and are performing well enough to be able to bargain for lower interest rates. That's what we ask of the banks, but rates continue to remain flat, and banks are reluctant to reduce them even if a group is performing well. When you talk to the bank about reducing interest rates, they ask for a guarantee fund. They tend to focus on the risk factor, and the higher the risk, the higher the interest.

These are challenges that we need to break through if our beneficiaries are to not only survive, but to thrive.

Remember Faustin, the ICT graduate who was so confident at graduation that he could start a viable business? Faustin and his fellow trainees wanted to open a cyber café, but their proposals to NGOs raised only 300,000 of the 4,000,000 Rwf (almost $5,000) needed. They could be offering a valuable service to camp residents today, but instead, Faustin makes a living by selling some of the items that are given to his family for free.

Gasana Alcade is another person that comes to mind when I think of exceptional refugees who have done well, but need a little more help to reach a higher level of self-reliance and success. Gasana has been at Kigeme Refugee Camp for about five years. During peaceful times in the DR Congo, he had farmland and cows, and he's now part of a group of twenty refugees who make soap to sell. His group wants to provide their soap to a much bigger market, including restaurants and hotels, but needs funds to purchase the right quantity of materials needed to scale up.

Unfortunately, we've experienced a declining number of people who want to be trained to learn new skills and start businesses, because they see that others who went before them, like Faustin and Gasana, are now stuck at a certain level.

Another group of concern are those who are creating products, but are frustrated because they don't have the ideal market. When they do manage to sell items, it is usually to locals, and they have to sell at a discouragingly low price. For refugees at the camps, and for the locals who also participate in **GHDF** programs, an increase in public awareness of what they create and what they do will lead to an increase in production and income. We are looking into ways to raise awareness about their products and services to potential buyers nationally, regionally, and internationally.

Sometimes substantial funding or a large upfront investment is what's needed to start a program or a business venture in a way that will give it the momentum to make a big impact and continue on its own. But another challenge we constantly face in the humanitarian field is that many donors are constrained to give you what they have instead of what is needed, and they'll ask you to work within their limits. We have to prioritize, but it's difficult. As an implementer on the ground, you're always in hot water because you're going to have to explain to the persons of concern why you decided to help only a few, or to help them only to a certain extent.

Other times, quick funding could make a big difference. There are times when NGOs submit proposals and end up spending almost a year without being funded. By the time the funding comes, the nature of the real problem has changed. Timely response is important because the magnitude of the problem keeps on growing with time. If this was a problem that was at ten percent and you don't sort it out early, in the next few months it raises to sixty percent. When we finally start to implement the program or plan that we proposed, it's not going to sort out any problem. Flexibility and dynamism are important, and would help us respond to the needs of the people instead of letting problems gain magnitude.

At GHDF, we do not let obstacles change our decision to reach our goal. We do not let a limited access to funds stop us from doing what is right. We may have to do things on a small scale for a while, but we have faith, we persevere, and we continue to search for ways to overcome. Our challenge and our goal is to support and sustain the livelihoods of our current groups in ways that will serve as a model for future beneficiaries and partners—not only in Rwanda, but also in low-income nations and in communities around the globe.

The SAFI story about how we stretched donor funds to multiply the number of beneficiaries in Gatsibo District—and thousands of other untold stories from the field—show us that given a chance, refugees and other vulnerable groups can learn new skills, and share what skills they already have, to improve their lives. They can be responsible, and make choices that will help them grow.

Time and time again, we have seen refugees and other disadvantaged individuals rise out of their circumstances, and in turn joyfully help others. They have an enthusiasm and a passion born of having been in the same boat, of knowing how it feels to be lifted out, and of wanting to give others a chance of a better life. I believe that no matter a person's station in life, they can rise to help themselves, and to lift others. This is the vision and the mission to which my staff and I have devoted our lives.

I was once a refugee myself, and instead of letting my experiences keep me down, I trusted in God, and I imagined and planned a better future that involves helping others. Maybe you have also overcome challenges and want to find a way to give back in a meaningful way. Or maybe you are currently going through the same kind of life and hardships that I went through in my younger days. If so, be strong and know that there is a purpose for your life. Circumstances can and do change, and the process often begins with your thoughts and intentions.

12

CALL TO ACTION

"The best way to not feel hopeless is to get up and do something. Don't wait for good things to happen to you. If you go out and make some good things happen, you will fill the world with hope, you will fill yourself with hope."

—President Barack Obama

One of the goals for Rwanda's Vision 2020 is to make Rwanda a middle-income country, and the work GHDF does with the economic empowerment programs and the Village Savings and Loans Associations all support that goal. The government supports everything NGOs do in response to the Economic Development and Poverty Reduction Strategy (EDPRS), and has helped us connect and work with local communities. By engaging us in policy-making at different levels through joint-action forums, the ground is prepared to encourage and enable us to support the people.

We have been part and parcel of several policies related to our work, including one that allows civil society organizations to invest in income-generating activities. We pushed for many years before the parliament finally approved it. Now, non-governmental organizations can do business to help support their programs and reduce their dependence on donors. This is important because donors are starting to ask us to show them what we have on the table before they bring anything out.

Beyond 2020 there will be a renewed vision, and additional areas to address. The work of helping those in need, as I mentioned before, will forever be in progress. It will take many hands and minds, through many generations, to build a nation—and eventually a world—where everyone is at their full potential. President Paul Kagame once expressed the nation's desire "to make the kind of progress that will make Rwanda unrecognizable to those who define us by our tragic history." Today, it's clear that that desire has already been fulfilled. Rwanda has made remarkable progress, but if we're to listen to my father's advice, we have to make it even better. There is always room for growth.

People sometimes ask which projects or achievements I'm most proud of, but it's hard to decide. I think almost every single project we've done has been successful because each person we helped or trained moved to higher standards of living. People who were once too poor to send their children to school now have small businesses and can afford basic education. People who once had no skills are proud to list all the things they can do, and all the ways they can serve. Out in the field, it's clear to see that we are changing and improving people's lives, but it's also clear to see that much more is needed.

In Uganda I watched my parents and the refugee community suffer for too long, never getting what they asked for—not from the host community and not from their own government. As a refugee child in desperate need, I expected my teacher in Buyongo to see and respond with kindness, giving me those school supplies I believed would change my life, but he did not. When I reflect on these experiences and many others, I know now that all these things had an effect on how I communicated—or did not communicate—my needs and my thoughts with others.

One important lesson I've learned on this journey from refugee to humanitarian leader is to speak up and be an advocate for even more powerful change. You can take the initiative to do something better by yourself, but motivating and persuading others to join your cause is often more powerful and effective. I also now believe that it is possible, even for an individual, to persuade a big institution to do the right thing.

As I end this account of my early years and my work, I want to acknowledge everyone who has supported the work of PAJER/GHDF in the past, and to highlight the areas in which we, together, can do even more meaningful and far-reaching things. I also want to invite people who are just learning about the Global Humanitarian and Development

Foundation for the first time to consider where you might fit in as partners on our mission, or how we may fit in as partners on yours. On the last page of this book you will find a list of ways to get involved, and you may reach out to me or to GHDF staff anytime at https://www.ghdf.org.rw

Our top goals for now, and in the near future, are vocational training and livelihoods. We want to close the gap for the many who did not have the chance to get a formal education. Giving people water and shelter in emergency situations is one thing, but helping them sustain their lives after that is perhaps the most critical of all. GHDF needs increased funding and wide support to do two things: First, expand our work to more beneficiaries who are in need, and second, help refugees move from the day-to-day dependence on aid to a more sustainable kind of life.

You don't have to be from a rich family to be able to do something good with your life. I was a fresh graduate from school, and from a poor family, when I made the decision to resign from my first job and start an organization to support youth and disadvantaged people. The point is that you don't need to know much or have a lot of money to do something good or to start a project. You don't need to be brilliant or from an elite or privileged family to make a difference. You don't have to be young either. Like my mother always said, everyone has something to offer. Everyone can experience the joy of giving and making an impact in someone else's life.

My father used to tell me to be responsible for everything—not only for things in my personal interest, but in the public's interest as well. "If you see something wrong," he would say, "do something about it or report it to someone who can. Be a Good Samaritan." Despite his own troubles back in Mukono, he was a community advocate who fought for justice for neighbors and friends who had been treated unfairly. He didn't have money, but he gave his time.

I've been asked if having to be responsible for everything ever felt like a burden, and the answer is no. It has never been a burden and never will be. I always feel that it's a personal commitment, and something that I just have to do. It becomes a burden if I *don't* do what needs to be done, and I feel completely uncomfortable if there is something that I know I had to do, and either didn't do it, or didn't do it the right way. Aline and I have six children now, and I am teaching them to always be responsible too, because it's very important.

If you haven't yet, start making an impact in your communities immediately. Being part of an initiative that supports people in need is critical to your growth, whether you are young or old. You don't need to acquire degrees or get special training first. Start now and you can begin to learn from experience, and shape a future that will bring you joy and fulfillment. It is a question of willingness and readiness.

Each of us was put on this earth for a purpose, and it's my sincere hope that, like me, you will clearly hear your calling and share in some way the talents and blessings that you have been given.

EPILOGUE

HOW TO GROW AS A LEADER AND HELP OTHERS RISE TO THEIR FULL POTENTIAL: SEVEN KEYS

My father always said that you could define your future if you had a clear path. I think what he meant is that if you know where you want to be, and you have a clear picture of what you want to achieve in life, then you can set clear objectives to reach milestones that will get you closer to realizing your dream. Getting clarity doesn't happen overnight, though. It may take you some time to figure out what you want, or what your life's purpose is. I suggest you have a goal, but be open to changing it as your perspectives change. Any path you set is vulnerable to sudden twists and turns as you experience different things in life. Those experiences change your perspectives, and in turn may change your goal. Create and re-create yourself and your purpose as often as necessary. Constantly strive to be a better person, and to do better. Take every opportunity to reach for better outcomes—for yourself and for others—than you initially hoped to have.

If you are just starting out, I suggest you do a self-assessment to determine your main interests and strengths. I also want to encourage you to consider how you can use your strengths to reach out to others while doing what you love. If you are already in the workforce or doing voluntary work, how can you be more effective and more fulfilled? How can you grow as a leader in your field and help others along the way?

If you care about the poor, and about people in need, there are many ways you can offer support. Individuals, churches and mosques, local organizations, the international development community, the business community, donor agencies—all of us have a role to play. There is nothing greater or nobler than supporting people in need, and it is a calling that some of us have heard in I Peter 4:10, which says *Each of you should use whatever gift you have received to serve others, as faithful stewards of God's grace in its various forms.*

What role can you play in your community or in your country? How can you incorporate serving others with the work you already do? If you already serve others in a humanitarian or development setting, how can you do it effectively? How can you be a true change agent?

Considering some of the critical lessons I've learned in our work at Global Humanitarian and Development Foundation, I have put together seven keys for success in helping individuals and communities rise to their full potential:

1. The Foundation of Success: Dream Big, Start Small

We have had success at GHDF, but I've also made mistakes, or had some challenges, as I prefer to say. One of those challenges I encountered came in the beginning, when I first got started as PAJER. I had big ambitions and thought it would be quick to move things, but by the end of the second year I was discouraged. I had spent two years without funding and couldn't understand why. I had a plan to start the debate program at the district level, move into the provincial level, and then move to the national level and organize major competitions. I thought donors would come running because it was a great idea. But when I was talking to them, they asked me, "Who are you? You have such a big plan but you have not done anything. How sure are we that you have the capacity to do all this?" That's when I decided to take smaller steps to establish myself. Instead of starting the debate program at the district level, I went to the schools—first in Kigali, and later in the rural areas.

Starting small allowed me to show people, including myself, what I could do. It allowed me to learn along the way, and to change course when an idea was not working as anticipated. You may have big dreams or a long-term vision, but start small. Learn from the mistakes you'll make on a daily basis. When you take a step forward and encounter a challenge, sit back and think about it, then solve it and move forward again. Starting small gives you a chance to grow from a solid foundation.

If your goal is to help people who are living in poverty, it's important to know that a little can go a long way. A baby learning to walk will take a step, fall down, take another step, fall down again, but with persistence he starts walking. Be consistent and work with people step by step, and understand that it's important to let your level of investment match with their growth. Once you get someone started, they will grow progressively from there.

2. Persevere or Perish: What it Takes to Overcome Obstacles

Commitment is more important than brilliance or experience. We have been able to accomplish many things in our humanitarian work even though we were not experts in every situation. The truth is that fieldwork does not require a lot of experience or an extensive academic background. It is all about listening to the people, understanding exactly what they want, and aligning your thoughts with their desires to make sure you come up with something that they own. In order for individuals and communities to grow, they need support from people who are committed, ready to listen, and ready to act.

Commitment is the ability to consistently do what you're supposed to do even if there are daunting challenges. If you have passion for something, or a dream you want to realize, do whatever it takes to keep moving until you get there. That is commitment. There will be ups and downs, and things won't always go as smoothly as you want, but be consistent and take steps to get your work done, and done right, no matter how much time it takes. When you are committed to fighting for what you or others truly want, you are much more likely to persevere and reach your goal.

3. Listen to the People!

For decades, individuals and organizations have been striving to eradicate poverty, but poor people in many parts of the world are still living in almost the same conditions as they did before interventions.

If you want your intervention to be effective, don't come and say, "I'm going to build a primary school here because I want to move you out of poverty." That's the mistake many NGOs and donor agencies make. Instead, talk to the people, and view situations from their perspectives. The way you define poverty may not be the way they define it. You may think that establishing a school in a village will end poverty, but the poor villagers may have a better solution. If you come and dictate to people who are in such a condition, they will keep quiet, and they might even attend the groundbreaking and clap their hands after your speech, but they won't attend that school. And the next year you'll ask, "Why is the enrollment so low? We thought this was your primary school program."

When the people you want to support come on board and are allowed to help with the design and planning of programs or projects, it's a different story. When we started our first micro-loan programs, we listened to input from the community and earned their trust and commitment. Beneficiaries came to meetings on time, and soon began managing themselves. At first, each person was saving a hundred Rwandan francs a week. Three months later, after they gained confidence in the program, they took a decision to increase the amount to five hundred francs a week because they knew that the higher the savings, the better the opportunity for large investment loans from the group.

Those groups managed their own resources and multiplied their result more than two or three times in the year. They owned the program, and our teams were behind them, simply listening and advising. What would take you five years to move people from one step to another would take so much less time if you let them take the lead. It would be cost effective too, because they don't need a lot of supervision if they do things themselves.

People may be poor in terms of resources, but they are not poor in terms of knowledge of what they want. All they need is for you to talk to them, and listen to them. Listening is an important strength. Before you do anything, do a baseline survey. Find out what their most pressing needs are. They will give you the priorities in order, and if you follow their priorities, you will move with them. If you don't, and instead think for them, you will move alone and you will waste your resources and your time.

4. Be Transparent About Your Capacity and Deliver on Your Promises

In our early days, when the Economic Empowerment Program was nothing but a dream, I went to Rwanda's Rulindo District with a debate program and afterwards talked to a large group of participants and local people who were eager for vocational training and micro-loans to support themselves. They had lots of good ideas about what they would do, and I promised I would sign on with a donor and soon return to give them what they wanted. I didn't know that making promises to the people before I had funds was wrong, and at the end of the day could cost me their trust.

Taking the advice of my wife, I went back to the district to apologize to the community. It was difficult to face them and know I had let them down, but they appreciated the update. Hearing the bad news was better than being left to wonder when or if I would ever come back, and hearing it from me enabled us to maintain a good relationship.

When we finally had funds to implement some projects, I went back to the same people I had disappointed and planned another project with them. It was two or three years later and their needs had changed, but there were other issues we were able to address together. I still have the confidence and trust of those people today.

Always be honest about what you can do, and follow through on what you say you'll do. Keep promises you make to others, and keep promises you make to yourself. You never want to be seen as someone who is making promises, and not fulfilling them.

5. Be An Exemplary Leader

A majority of our funding has come as a result of approaching donors and building relationships. One donor representative told me, "I'm not giving money to organizations. I'm giving money to individuals in those organizations." When I asked her to explain, she said: "We have given organizations a lot of funding, but in the end, many of them failed us. However, when I meet you in person, it's about interviewing you and understanding if you have the capacity to utilize the funding that we are talking about. I need to see if you have the capacity as a manager to implement a program."

As we discussed further, I realized that she was right. If a donor talks to the head of the organization, and sees that he or she has the capacity to implement, then they can be more confident that promises will be kept. You have to talk to potential donors first, and try to create relationships. Let them get to know you, the organization you work for, and your experience.

The reputation of the leader of an organization is extremely important. One of the challenges is to link the verbal trust and the real activity on the ground. You may leave the initial donor meeting having spoken sweet words and convinced them you have the capacity to do many things, but what happens when they get you on board? Do you end up doing less than what was expected? That is the biggest challenge that both sides face. I invest a lot of energy in talking to donors, then when they believe in me and give me funding for our programs, the pressure is on to prove beyond a reasonable doubt that I was the right person for the job. But if you talk sweet words and you don't implement, then it comes across as the donor's bad choice.

Another challenge donors face is that they may trust a leader who ends up leaving. They funded you, but you're sitting there and someone calls and says, "There's a good job in Kenya. They want a Deputy Representative and you would be so good. Why don't you apply?" Then you apply and get the job. The trust that has been invested in you and the organization is now at risk. The person who takes your place may be completely different from you and may not want to serve in the same way.

Donors ask themselves: "Within the project lifespan, will this person that we have trusted be there?" If you want to be an exemplary leader, be committed to seeing your projects through. Twice in recent years I have been offered high-paying jobs that would have solved some personal problems for me, but I declined because I did not want to divert myself from the GHDF mission. Mine is a purpose-driven life and God has guided me all the way from day one to today. I believe that leaving what I am doing today would be breaking a promise and the commitment I made to God and to the people I was meant to help.

Exemplary leaders must also plan well. If you do too-little planning, though you have been trusted, you won't achieve the project output. Trust grows with time. Every time you finish a cycle and you do it well, you can see that you're more welcomed, and you're more respected. When you finish a cycle and move from one project to another, you might also see growth in terms of funding levels.

Finally, for whatever role you play, you need to know your strengths and your weaknesses as an individual, and as an organization if applicable. How have you improved over time? That matters a lot, and you must continuously assess yourself and grow from your findings.

6. Stay Humble

Staying humble is difficult, especially when you are in a position where you have to talk about yourself and your accomplishments. There are times that you'll see your efforts are working out, and you're making progress. You are helping people in need, but you end up focusing on the gains you're making, and the success. People see you like a small god sometimes. They praise you because they are poor and you have moved them forward. And then you start thinking you are not a normal human being, that you are someone who is supernatural, someone who is different. The moment you do that, the moment you see what you have done as an achievement that not many have done, and you think you've reached a certain caliber or you should now move up to a higher level of class, that is the beginning of the end.

How do you not change? How do you keep yourself grounded? As a Christian, I look at what Jesus did—feeding multitudes, healing the sick, raising Lazarus from the dead, and so much more. What he did, no one else could have done, and no one else has ever done. But Jesus stayed the same person until he died. He did not change. He walked with his disciples all the way. Because of what he was doing, he could have become a king and he could have sat there on a throne and everyone around the world would have believed in him. But Jesus kept his focus on God. He prayed and sought guidance from God. He saw his Father in everyone—in those who loved him and in those who persecuted him. He performed miracles, but he knew there was still a lot of work to be done.

I can never do what Jesus did, but in my capacity, I look back at where I came from, and acknowledge my dependence on God. No matter how much you've accomplished, stay outwardly focused because needs are always there, and you have not achieved enough to take all those needs away. You have done a little bit, but you haven't achieved it all. It's work in progress. To illustrate: If you're working on a dissertation and your director says the first chapter is excellent, you should not start celebrating because there are many chapters to come that might be more difficult to write. Humanitarian and development work is always work in progress. I will do my part, others will do their part, and it goes on and on. No matter how much you've done, it is never enough, and it is never finished. To stay humble, begin each day expressing gratitude to God, and end each day giving Him the glory for all that was achieved.

7. Plan for Growth and Sustainability

It's important to plan sustainability for your business or organization, and also for the programs that the entity implements. That should go hand in hand. I created GHDF many years ago, and we have done only a portion of the work that is supposed to be done. If I die tomorrow morning and the organization crumbles or completely closes, then I have failed. The primary goal of this organization is to serve people in need, so making sure the organization will survive even without me is my ultimate goal. Much as someone can be impressed with the work we are doing, the most important impression that anyone could have would be to see someone else at the helm long after I have left this office.

How do we plan sustainability?

Sustainability has to start from the activities on the ground, where everything you do should contribute to the growth of all the individuals involved. Keep track of what you are doing and make sure you know the true needs of the people you are serving. Listen to them, know what they want, and help them. Make it easy for them to reach their goals, and even without you they will keep on working. They will keep on moving forward.

When I talk about sustainability for GHDF specifically, we have put structures in place for a transition, and we are continuously strengthening within so that the organization can work without me and survive through subsequent leaders. We are closing knowledge gaps for those who are already in the organization, and making sure the key staff is strong. We also want a Board of experts who will make themselves available to the staff.

Another way to ensure sustainability is by advocating for long-term programs rather than short-term projects. Long-term is anywhere from three to five years. If a project is funded for only one or two years, that time is often not enough to leave the beneficiaries with enough maturity and maximum impact. One urban microfinance project we started worked for only eight months and then collapsed, because that was the length of the donations. The long-term programs that we conducted—those with funding for three to five years—are still running and even expanding by themselves. It is what we call internal growth. They are expanding by themselves because we had enough time with the beneficiaries. We gave them the necessary training and the capacity building for a good amount of time. Short-term programs often don't make enough of an impact, and are sometimes a waste of resources.

To truly help people and organizations for the long-term, planning for sustainability is key. Build the capacity of volunteers and staff, share the tasks or pass the baton to others who share your vision, and, even as you're making day-to-day impact, think of what could be accomplished in the long term. Planning for sustainability begins with the first key in helping individuals and communities reach their full potential, and should be kept in mind as you pay attention to all the others.

To recap, here are the seven keys to success in your efforts to help others rise to their full potential:

1. Dream Big, Start Small
2. Persevere or Perish
3. Listen to the People
4. Be Transparent About Your Capacity and Deliver on Your Promises
5. Be an Exemplary Leader
6. Stay Humble
7. Plan for Growth and Sustainability

Without the first six of these keys, planning for growth and sustainability may prove to be a fruitless exercise. Incorporating all seven of them into your chosen path will certainly illuminate your way.

I've sacrificed a lot to do what I do, and there was a period of over a decade when I did not make time to go out for a break with my family. I didn't take holidays, and I was getting home close to or after midnight almost every day. But despite my absences from home, my wife was always supportive. While you may become ambitious about serving others and take on the never-ending task of changing the world, please know that I've since learned about the importance of balancing work and family. I am at home more often, and we finally took a long overseas family vacation together a couple of years ago. Much as you have your loved ones on board and think you are doing a wonderful job, it's a primary responsibility to have time for your family.

When you value what you do, you may spend many hours at work moving things forward, but your family needs your presence. Always secure some time for the family.

My wife has been part of this journey from the beginning, and she has been instrumental in how far we have gone with the organization. She has spent time handling paperwork, sitting and conceptualizing ideas with the Board of Directors, and giving strategy direction in partnership with members of the Board. She has been deeply involved in every single bit of the work I do, so I believe my success is hers too. Besides giving both moral and organizational support, she is the incredible force that sustains our home and makes it a joy for our children.

I miss my parents, and wish they could have lived to see my siblings and I developing our own visions and our own paths to achieving our dreams. I am proud to be raising my children in their own country, and will forever pay tribute to my parents for making sure we knew our culture, and that someday we would know our home.

I plan to continue the example of my father and my mother by passing lessons on to my children. Both of my parents played an enormous role in what I've done and in who I am today. They sacrificed and invested in me and my siblings so that we would have moral values, and know how to use our knowledge wisely. For the most part, all my siblings and I have overcome various struggles and are thriving and doing the best we can for our families and our communities.

I'm a product of my parents, and I would love for my children to embody the things that Aline and I are teaching them. I would love to see them not only thinking about their lives and their own development, but also thinking about how they might impact the lives of others. I would love to see my children being humble, being passionate about something, and thinking about how they can make the world better than they found it. We sometimes think children are too young to understand, but if you engage them, as my parents engaged me, they understand and they'll never forget.

I want my children to leave a legacy behind at the end of the day. I want to encourage you to leave a legacy behind at the end of the day. I want each of you reading this book to be remembered as someone who answered a noble calling to do something better and make a difference in people's lives.

Me with our two sons.

Aline with our three oldest daughters.

ACKNOWLEDGMENTS

To my late grandparents who supported my early childhood development: I owe you a great debt, and will always keep you in my prayers of gratitude.

To my late parents, John Kalegesa and Madeleine Mukandekezi, who did everything they could to help me realize a better future: Thank you for being an inspiration to our family. I will always practice and represent the human values you invested in us.

To my supportive and beloved wife, Aline Kaneza, and our six wonderful children: Without your love, care, and support, it would not have been possible to write this book. I am so grateful to you.

I would also like to express my sincere gratitude to Dr. Alan Graustein, Dr. Rick Bonifas, Elma Shaw, and all of you who have contributed to the production of this book.

Finally, heartfelt appreciation goes to my friends and colleagues who have immensely contributed to the vision and mission of GHDF. You have been walking with me all the way from the beginning, and, because of your support, there are many once-destitute people who can now imagine a better future. Thank you, and may the Almighty Lord be with you always.

ABOUT THE AUTHOR

Patrick Karangwa has been motivating young people to make the world a better place for over two decades. Born in Uganda during his parents' exile, he moved to his native Rwanda in 1995. His experiences growing up as a refugee led him to a life dedicated to peacemaking and service to others. While attending the Kigali Institute of Education, where he earned a teaching degree, Karangwa co-founded the Student Club for Unity and Reconciliation (SCUR). In 2000, he established the Rwanda Youth Parliament (PAJER) to promote peace and unity through debate and dialogue, and to provide people with skills training and micro-loans for economic empowerment. Now known as the Global Humanitarian and Development Foundation (GHDF), the organization is also active in refugee camps and local communities, serving tens of thousands of vulnerable people from Rwanda and neighboring countries. Karangwa has an Executive MBA from Mount Kenya University, and is the CEO of GHDF. He lives in Kigali with his wife, Aline Kaneza, and their children.

TO GET INVOLVED WITH GHDF...

If there is something good in you that you can share with others, it makes sense to do so. They will be transformed, and so will you. What are your interests? Is there something you're already passionate about? How do you serve? How do you want to serve? The world needs your good heart and your generous hand.

If you are interested in humanitarian and development work, there are several ways to get involved with the Global Humanitarian and Development Foundation:

- You can become a GHDF volunteer.

- You can become a financial supporter with a one-time or a monthly gift. Many of our beneficiaries need only a little help to be able to get to the next level, while others need a bigger investment.

- Students may start a GHDF University Club or a GHDF Secondary School Club to raise awareness, clothing, books, and funds for the work we do with young refugees.

- Our online market for Agaseke baskets, jewelry, and other products made by people in our economic empowerment programs can be found at https://www.agasekeshop.com, and a percentage of the proceeds from any items purchased will support not just the artisans, but their extended families as well.

- GHDF has many opportunities for partnership, and some of the things we do—like the innovative latrines and the VSLAs—can be applied outside of Rwanda and even outside of Africa. Please contact us to discuss ideas for collaboration.

- To find out more about our work and explore the ways you can get involved, please visit our website at https://www.ghdf.org.rw.